"This is *the* book that addresses the subtle nuances of effective exposure-based treatment that most self-help books overlook. She explains common misunderstandings that undermine progress, such as resisting checking to prove nothing bad will happen—as opposed to resisting checking to exercise the 'welcoming' muscles that build resilience and confidence in the face of uncertainty."

—**Sally Winston, PsyD**, coauthor of *Needing to Know for Sure* and *Overcoming Unwanted Intrusive Thoughts*

"Wow! Jennifer Shannon brings thirty exercises—one month's worth—to help you become more accepting of the uncertainty that exists all around us. The aim isn't to abolish, or even master, uncertainty—it's to acclimate, and even take pleasure in feelings of not being in control, because that's what life is all about. If you want more flexibility, joy, and peace in your life, this book is for you. Too busy for daily exercises? This book is especially for you!"

—**Dave Carbonell, PhD**, "coach" on the popular self-help site, www.anxietycoach.com; and author of *Panic Attacks Workbook*, *The Worry Trick*, *Fear of Flying Workbook*, and *Outsmart Your Anxious Brain*

T0120353

"Think of *The Monkey Mind Workout for Uncertainty* as your mental boot camp, in the best sense of the term. Jennifer Shannon makes a bold promise: to reshape our attitude toward the inevitable uncertainties of the future. And then she delivers, using powerful, playful guidance to help us take immediate action, break our usual patterns, and do things differently. Simple and bold, quick and user-friendly, this set of structures will help you cut a clear path to the joys of being flexible, curious, and at peace."

—**Reid Wilson, PhD**, author of *Stopping the Noise in Your Head*

"*The Monkey Mind Workout for Uncertainty* is a welcome addition to our worried world, with helpful tips and engaging stories to build resilience in the face of uncertainty. I am excited to recommend this book to my readers and friends, particularly those who struggle with generalized anxiety or the need to feel in control."

—**Arlin Cuncic, MA**, author of *The Anxiety Workbook*, and founder of www.aboutsocialanxiety.com

"Both brilliant and fun! A humor-filled workout for dealing with uncertainty is just what we need right now. If you struggle with anxiety, decision-making, or feel pain when things can't be 'just so, ' this program is sure to help. I loved the inspirational, comical drawings and daily creative exercises for embracing uncertainty, building self-compassion and resilience, and finding more joy in life. Sweating the small stuff never felt so good."

—**Christine A. Padesky, PhD**, clinical psychologist, coauthor of *Mind Over Mood*, and author of *The Clinician's Guide to CBT Using Mind Over Mood*

"This delightful book is just what you need to help your brain and body learn to tolerate the discomfort of uncertainty. Written with a bright, positive, and upbeat style—at times quite personal—Jennifer Shannon will guide you through 'workouts' that are manageable, scientifically valid, and can be tooled to your own particular needs."

—**Martin N. Seif, PhD, ABPP**, cofounder of the Anxiety and Depression Association of America (ADAA); and coauthor of *What Every Therapist Need to Know About Anxiety Disorders, Overcoming Unwanted Intrusive Thoughts,* and *Needing to Know for Sure*

THE
MONKEY
MiND
WORKOUT FOR

UNCERTAINTY

BREAK FREE *from* ANXIETY &
BUILD RESILIENCE *in* 30 DAYS!

JENNIFER SHANNON, LMFT
Illustrations by **DOUG SHANNON**

New Harbinger Publications, Inc.

Publisher's Note

Distributed in Canada by Raincoast Books

Copyright © 2022 by Jennifer Shannon
New Harbinger Publications, Inc.
5674 Shattuck Avenue
Oakland, CA 94609
www.newharbinger.com

Illustrations by Doug Shannon

Cover design by Amy Shoup; Acquired by Tesilya Hanauer;
Edited by Jean Blomquist

Library of Congress Cataloging-in-Publication Data

Names: Shannon, Jennifer, author.
Title: The monkey mind workout for uncertainty : break free from anxiety & build
    resilience in 30 days! / Jennifer Shannon, LMFT.
Description: Oakland, CA : New Harbinger Publications, [2020]
Identifiers: LCCN 2020004668 (print) | LCCN 2020004669 (ebook) | ISBN
    9781684035885 (paperback) | ISBN 9781684035892 (pdf) | ISBN 9781684035908
    (epub)
Subjects: LCSH: Anxiety--Treatment. | Cognitive therapy--Popular works.
Classification: LCC RC531 .S443 2020 (print) | LCC RC531 (ebook) | DDC
    616.85/22--dc23
LC record available at https://lccn.loc.gov/2020004668
LC ebook record available at https://lccn.loc.gov/2020004669

Printed in the United States of America

24   23   22

10   9   8   7   6   5   4   3   2   1   First Printing

Contents

Foreword   v

Introduction   1

The Big One   3

A Must-Be-Certain State of Mind   7

Feeding the Monkey   15

Resilience   21

The Workout   27

   1. Welcoming Warm-Up   33

   2. Count Your Check'ns   38

   3. Curb the Urge   41

   4. Lose Your Health Assurance   45

   5. Pace, Don't Race   50

   6. Take a Taste Test   53

   7. Step on a Crack   57

   8. Can't Remember? Let It Be   60

   9. Take the Road Less Traveled   64

  10. Decide to Declutter   69

  11. Get Off the Clock   73

12. Don't Feed on News Feeds   78

13. Go Without a Net   82

14. Don't Double-Check   86

15. Choose a Random Queue   90

16. Go on a Social Media Diet   95

17. If This, Then That   98

18. Underplan, Underprepare!   102

19. Throw Caution, Not Food, To the Wind   106

20. Forget About It   110

21. Make a Quick Decision   114

22. Go Off the Grid   119

23. Loosen Grip on Loved Ones   123

24. Rock Your Routine   128

25. Recognize Reassurance Seeking   131

26. Reduce Reassurance Seeking   136

27. Shuffle Your Deck   140

28. Don't DIY, Delegate!   144

29. Flip a Coin   148

30. Welcome a Worry   153

Epilogue   157

Foreword

Years ago, my wife and I were deep into a major home remodel that included adding a second floor. We were working with a wonderful architect who asked to meet with us prior to our meeting with a structural engineer that the architect had hired. The engineer would make recommendations for strengthening the house in order to safely support the second-floor addition during an earthquake.

As the architect, my wife, and I huddled around a small table in the kitchen, the architect said, "If you ask a structural engineer to recommend a house that will be safest in an earthquake, the engineer will tell you that the safest house is one without doors and windows. The engineer will tell you that each time you add a door, either inside or outside, or a window, you weaken the structure. Each door and each window you add will increase risk because you're a little less certain that the structure will handle the rocking and rolling of a big earthquake. Now," the architect continued, "if you want to be more certain and therefore a bit safer, follow the engineer's advice. Eliminate all the doors and windows in your house and don't add new ones. In the end, you'll have a safer house, but it will be a house without light and doors. I have two questions for you, 'Do you want to live in a house without light? Do you want to live in a house that you can't leave?'"

If you answered no to the architect's question, as we did, then this new book by Jennifer Shannon is for you. *The Monkey Mind Workout for Uncertainty*, the first of a three-book series, teaches powerful cognitive behavioral skills that will help you manage your anxious, chattering, and annoying monkey mind. Fittingly, Jennifer begins the series with uncertainty. It's uncertainty that makes us anxious—you, me, and Jennifer—but here's the thing. You can't avoid uncertainty, although you can make peace with it, and this book can help you do just that.

The Monkey Mind Workout for Uncertainty begins by introducing the relationship between uncertainty and anxiety and the costs of a futile pursuit of certainty at all costs. This "must-be-certain mind-set," as Jennifer points out, feeds the anxious monkey mind and fosters intolerance to one of the inescapable facts of life: life is uncertain. Once you understand the costs of rejecting uncertainty and the anxiety that accompanies it, Jennifer presents thirty exercises that will build your tolerance to uncertainty. Do these thirty exercises—one exercise each day—and in a month, you'll feel less anxious. That may seem too good to be true, but the exercises make use of well-tested cognitive behavioral techniques. Through each exercise, you'll practice stepping into uncertainty. You'll step on a crack to practice tolerating the uncertainty that accompanies superstitious beliefs. You'll take the road less traveled to practice tolerating the uncertainty that accompanies novelty. Several of the exercises involve your smartphone, and you'll practice untethering from a device that provides the illusion of certainty but fuels anxiety instead. There are many more, and each and every one of them is fun and effective.

Do not assume, however, that because Jennifer presents the exercises in a playful way that she isn't serious. Jennifer has a bit of a monkey mind herself, and she knows firsthand the power of the exercises she'll teach you. In fact, she's practiced all thirty exercises and what she's learned will inspire you. With practice, you'll learn the deep lessons she's learned about the power of accepting the uncertainties that are part and parcel of a life well lived.

As you practice the thirty exercises in this book, you'll feel less anxious about the uncertainties you face in life too. As you make peace with uncertainty, your life will change. Your life will fill with light and space. That's the bargain we make with life: more uncertainty for more light.

—Michael A. Tompkins, PhD, ABPP
Author, *Anxiety and Avoidance: A Universal Treatment for Anxiety, Panic, and Fear*
Codirector, San Francisco Bay Area Center for Cognitive Therapy
Assistant Clinical Professor of Psychology, University of California, Berkeley

Introduction

After more than two decades of clinical work with anxiety, I often say that I am still my favorite client. That's because I've found that the same strategies that I use to help people with anxiety disorders can help anybody become more relaxed and confident, including me. Whether clinically anxious or everyday anxious, everyone is wired the same way. All anxiety is characterized by one or more of three unrealistic mind-sets:

1. Intolerance of uncertainty: "What I don't know or can't control is dangerous."

2. Perfectionism: "I must not make a mistake."

3. Over-responsibility: "I am responsible for others' happiness and safety."

The exercises in this book are focused on the first of these three, *intolerance of uncertainty*. While perfectionism and over-responsibility are serious problems for many, and other books in this series will address them, intolerance of uncertainty is the most common of these mind-sets. It's so deeply ingrained in our culture that it's considered normal. Our inability to cope with what is beyond our direct knowledge and control—what we can't be certain about—is the single biggest obstacle to our personal growth and happiness. To help you determine how tolerant of uncertainty you are, take my *Intolerance of*

Uncertainty Quiz downloadable at http://www.monkeymind books.com/u.

As you might guess from the word "workout" in the title, the exercises in this book are not only cognitive exercises. They are *behavioral* exercises, each of which will make us more resilient to the feelings and emotions that arise when we are faced with uncertainty. Only when we are resilient to everything, including the unknown, can we experience the confidence and peace we all crave and deserve!

The Big One

Living on a California fault line, my husband and I have contended with the possibility of an earthquake for years. We buttoned down everything in our home—self-locking cabinets, pictures hung with safety hooks, lamps and vases secured with museum putty. We hosted earthquake preparedness parties for our neighbors, slept with safety helmets and flashlights under the bed, and kept a shed on the back deck stocked with a week's worth of food and water. Then, only a few months after we retrofitted our foundation to better withstand the "big one," something big arrived.

Shortly before 1 a.m. on Monday, October 9, 2017, we were awakened by my ringing cell phone. It was a friend shouting, "You need to get out of there!" I knew instantly that he was right. The house was completely dark, electricity off, and I felt an acid bite of smoke in my throat. Frantically pulling on the clothes we'd taken off just a few hours earlier, we raced down the stairs for the family photos. That was all we had time for; pulling out of the garage, our headlights barely penetrated the smoke. As we inched toward the exit of our condominium complex, we could see a wall of crimson approaching through the trees. We later learned that less than an hour later our home was burned to the ground. Were it not for our friend's timely warning, my husband and I might never have woken up.

Never Again

Over 5,000 homes burned in the Tubbs fire. A combination of faulty wiring, dry weather, and 70 mph winds created a wildfire that traveled twelve miles in less than three hours, taking emergency crews and citizens by surprise. So many things went wrong that afterward a lot of people were asking, "How can we make sure nothing like this ever happens again?" While this was an important question, and I was grateful to those addressing it, I knew from my years of clinical work with anxiety disorders that preventing future disasters wasn't the only, or most important, challenge ahead. I'd seen too many clients who devoted themselves to anticipating and preventing the worst that could happen in the future, only to find themselves unhappy and exhausted in the present. And any illusions of certainty about my own future that I was harboring had just gone up in smoke. Our condo was equipped with commercial fire alarms and smoke detectors, and we were signed up for a wildfire warning system. They all failed. No matter how carefully we try to prevent disasters, we can be blindsided by those we don't anticipate.

In the weeks after the fire as I emerged from the shock, I felt the familiar tug of worry and tension creeping into my daily life. There were countless new tasks for me— clothing to buy, shelter to procure, insurance claims to file, records to replace— all the things necessary to put my life in order again. I'm a natural born planner, self-disciplined and persistent, and I had a partner and plenty of supporting friends, so I knew these things would get done. But I had no illusion that completing those tasks would keep me safe. And of course, I was right. Two years later, as this book is in page proofs, another big one, the coronavirus, has arrived, with a financial crisis appearing in its wake. With our growing realization of the omnipresent potential of loss, how can any of us feel confident and relaxed, not to mention joyful, again?

A Must-Be-Certain State of Mind

How many times have we sat, perhaps with a self-help book in our lap and a cup of tea in hand, promising to ourselves that we will relax our tight grip on life? Once and for all, we commit ourselves to stop sweating the small stuff, to stop worrying and be happy, to go with the flow. Perhaps we imagine ourselves in a virtual retreat, a quiet place where we won't be disturbed—*a peaceful setting like a tropical beach*—where we can watch our ruminations, plans, and worries float by like clouds. Here in the ordered sanctuary of our minds, we think, is where we can launch a new way of being. Whether it is making agreements with or daring ourselves, repeating positive affirmations and mantras, identifying our archetype, or mindfully meditating, we blaze new neurological pathways in our brains. When we emerge from our cocoons, we will flutter away free as butterflies.

Then, a few minutes or hours later, suddenly there is a traffic jam ahead. *Damn, I'm going to be late!* Or perhaps our text goes unanswered. *Did she arrive safely?* Maybe we notice a new spot on our arm or a pain in our gut. *Could it be cancer?* Or we read that alarming newsfeed. *If this is a market crash, do I have enough saved for retirement?* Suddenly the flow we were going with is pulling us into a sinkhole of "what ifs." The promises, resolutions, and agreements we made with ourselves are forgotten. The positive affirmations we tell ourselves ring hollow. What we dared greatly to imagine feels far too daunting to execute. Our peaceful state of mindfulness flips into mindless acting out. Before we are even aware of what we are doing, we are hitting the gas or reaching for our smartphone to text that loved one, check the time, google cancer symptoms, or monitor the condition of our 401(k).

These innocent little behaviors are symptomatic of the most common condition I see in my psychotherapy practice, in my friends and family, and in myself. It is so widespread that it is considered normal. This condition is *intolerance of uncertainty*, a state of mind and body that cannot bear the inherent unpredictability of life. When uncertainty is intolerable, we are continually occupied with the three Ps: planning, preparing, and prevention. We are always looking ahead, imagining the variables, and how we might prevent the worst from happening, or at least avoid its worst effects.

Consider the following four statements. How true do they sound to you?

1. Not knowing what lies ahead is dangerous.

2. I always need to be sure that I and others I care about are safe.

3. If things don't go as planned, my day is ruined.

4. I must always be on guard to prevent the worst from happening.

These are the unconscious assumptions of the *I-must-be-certain* mind-set, an obsessive way of thinking that prompts compulsive action that keeps us busy and unsatisfied. Saddled with the need to be certain, we are like racehorses wearing blinders: continually focused on the track ahead. *What might happen next and how can I control it?* Any rest we may hope for is contingent on our crossing the finish line of certainty.

And, of course, in a world where the only constant is change, we never truly arrive. Should we reach one milestone of certainty, before we can unharness ourselves, a new uncertainty appears on the horizon. By worrying, checking, planning, and manipulating our way through the day and half the night, is it any wonder we are emotionally exhausted, relying on alcohol, drugs, food, and media screens to dumb and numb us down?

Lost Values

Exhausting as the *I-must-be-certain* mind-set is, that is not its worst feature. Our need for certainty, because it requires us to pursue predictability and safety above everything else, has the crippling side effect of undermining our higher aspirations. Consider the following.

When we are rigidly attached to the plans we've made—certainty—we cannot be flexible when changing conditions require it. When we consistently seek situations where our tried-and-true behavior can be relied on—certainty—we never need to be creative. When we are comfortable only with our predictable routine—certainty—we cannot indulge our curiosity or be spontaneous when a fresh opportunity arises. When we interpret stress as an indication that we must work harder to eliminate what is stressing us—certainty—then we are never at peace. When we prefer fixed agendas with no surprises—certainty again!—we're not going to be much fun, are we? Any joy and celebration we might allow ourselves must wait until our future is properly planned and executed. Don't hold your breath!

The ability to be flexible, to be creative, curious, and spontaneous, to feel joy and be at peace are the attributes that make our lives worth living. Yet these values are the casualties of our pursuit of certainty. When we cannot tolerate uncertainty, we must avoid situations where we can't control the outcome—the very situations that require us to be flexible, where spontaneity and creativity are called for, and where pacing ourselves (knowing when to rest) is necessary. And it is in situations outside our control, in the wild flow of life, where our curiosity is most rewarded and where the greatest joys and deepest peace are to be discovered.

The pursuit of certainty is futile and exhausting, keeping us worried and stressed. It hinders the realization of our higher aspirations. And, because it steers us toward familiar situations where we know there will be a happy ending, we don't learn how to cope with open-ended, challenging situations. Our efforts to stay invulnerable keep us developmentally stunted and, ironically, more vulnerable to threats to our well-being. It is no wonder that we feel so insecure!

I make a promise in this book to help you break free from anxiety and build resilience, which is another way of saying to be relaxed and confident. But when we examine our tenuous jobs, our unpredictable state of health, our evolving relationships, our volatile economy, our unstable political scene and besieged environment, can we be confident about any of them long enough for us to relax?

Saddled with our *I-must-be-certain* mind-set, the only confidence we've known has been during the precious few moments of our lives when our plans have worked out and our future looked buttoned down and safe. What we need is a different kind of confidence altogether, a confidence that holds true even as we are faced with threatening possibilities beyond our knowledge and control. We need confidence that most of the unknown outcomes in our lives will be resolved favorably without our intervention, and that we can cope if they are not. Only when we are confident we can cope with the future, *any* future, can we relax now in this moment. How can we get this kind of confidence?

Feet on the Ground

Have you ever wanted to apply for a job that seemed perfect for you, except that it required two years of experience you didn't have, or a degree you hadn't acquired, or fluency in computer applications you'd never worked with? Our problem here is the same. To feel confident that we can cope with whatever lies ahead, we must have experience at coping. For some, this is a conundrum never to be resolved, but if you are determined to know the personal peace that is your birthright, this is an opportunity to take the next step in your evolution as a human being. If experience is required for you to grow, you can get that experience using the simple exercises in this book.

What I am saying is, all the insights, promises, affirmations, and meditations you've employed while sitting in the comfort of a quiet place are merely preparation for the action plan I am presenting here. Uncertainty must be welcomed not only in the space between our ears, but with our feet on the ground. We must purposely step into situations that we cannot control, where we can learn to cope and, with practice, come to feel confident that uncertainty is manageable for us. This workout will give you the type of new experience you need to build your resilience to uncertainty, which will enable you to think confidently and feel relaxed.

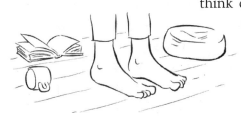 Only new experience will make an old mind-set die, and make a new one stick.

If we want to stop yearning for our aspirations and start living them, we must relax our grip on the future and greet it with an open hand of welcoming. Most of us understand this already, though perhaps not in these words exactly. Yet despite our good intentions to change our behavior, the moment we close our self-help books, or leave the therapist's office, or get up from our meditation pillow, we are triggered by one unknown or another, and we return once again to our old habits of planning, worrying, checking, and doing everything we can to alleviate our uncertain state of mind. What is the reason for this disconnect between how we yearn to be in the world and how we *behave* in the world? I'll answer that in detail in the next chapter, but here's the short version: we can make up our minds to welcome uncertainty, but our *emotions* have a mind of their own.

Feeding the Monkey

Have you ever had this thought about someone? *Oh, he'll never change.* Have you ever thought that about yourself? Once we become adults, most of us don't change very much. There's a good reason why even when we decide to "think differently," our actions tend to stay the same. When our survival is at stake, we can't afford to go changing our behavior willy-nilly. And to our *limbic system*, our survival is always at stake.

The limbic system is a complex network of nerves that reaches everywhere in our body, but is run by a cluster of brain structures, including the amygdala and hypothalamus, at the top of our brainstem. Our long-term memories are stored there—not only our personal life experience but also the collective lessons learned by the ancestors that came before us, passed along in our DNA. Using this previous experience as a reference, it screens everything in our path for signs of opportunity and threat, and then alerts us accordingly with either pleasant *rest-and-digest* feelings or unpleasant *fight-or-flight* feelings, including what we think of as emotions.

This virtual security guard does a terrific job of identifying imminent threats it has seen before, but in unfamiliar situations its perception is cloudy. Unlike the prefrontal cortex, where reasoning, cross-comparisons, and calculations are done, this part of our brain cannot perform risk assessment. It relies on instinctive guesses. For example, the sound of thunder can startle us, despite the fact our statistical chance of being hit by lightning is miniscule. For those of us with the *I-must-be-certain* mind-set, when it guesses—and in an ever-changing world of unknowns, it is often guessing—the guesses usually err on the side of safety. It overestimates the threat and underestimates our ability to cope, leaving us worried and tense much of the time, despite the fact that we currently enjoy better health and longevity than humans have at any other time in history.

The Monkey's Finger

What is essential to remember is that because this emotional brain-within-our-brain is below the level of our consciousness, it is beyond our direct control. It is a part of you, but it is not *you*. As such, we can conceptualize it a few different ways. Neurologists view it as a complex system to be mapped, monitored, and manipulated. Some analysts might view it as the unconscious, a void to be probed and interpreted. Others think of it as a computer program to be upgraded or hacked. It could also be thought of as the lower brain, something to be lifted up more to the level of the higher one you're reading this with.

All these analogies are helpful in their own ways, but in my practice and in my teaching, I have found that we can work with the limbic system most effectively when we recognize its animal nature. Since it is primitive and can be wildly undisciplined, has a lightning quick reaction time, and, as I said earlier, has, in effect, a mind of its own that is focused solely on survival, I have adopted the time-tested metaphor of the *monkey mind*. While it may sound whimsical, I do not suggest that we take it lightly. To enforce its survival agenda, this critter has its hairy finger on the fight-or-flight button of our autonomic nervous system. When the monkey mind says *jump*, we jump!

As a result, many of us live with regular low-level doses of fight-or-flight negative emotions, which keep us in a near-constant state of crisis. Life feels like a never-ending series of threatening problems to solve. We cannot relax when we feel as if our very survival depends on our staying on task. Being flexible is difficult when our feelings tell us we must

be faithful to our plans. We can't feel spontaneous or joyful when we feel afraid for our health, our livelihood, or our loved ones' well-being. So long as we are uncertain about what lies ahead, the monkey's finger is on the button, making us worried and stressed, enforcing the monkey mind-set *I-must-be-certain*.

This is our dilemma. No matter how much willpower we devote to accepting the unknown, when faced with the unknown, we will likely *feel* as if we are under threat. Fight-or-flight sensations like sweating, rapid heartbeat, shallow breathing, and stomach tension, as well as negative emotions like fear, irritability, and anger are the monkey's call to action. *Woo-woo-woo! Something is wrong! Do something!* With our body stuck in fight-or-flight mode, our brilliant executive brain—which does its best work when we are rest-and-digest mode— gets hijacked. In an instant, we're back to worrying, checking, and using distracting behaviors designed to avoid or control the perceived threat. We're picking up our phones to check on loved ones for reassurance that they are safe and our connection will continue, checking our social media to make sure we are still liked and followed, monitoring our news and sports feeds for reassurance whether our political party or team is going to win, and distracting ourselves with whatever "bright shiny object" is within our line of sight.

And these behaviors do work for us. When the monkey mind perceives that we are working on or avoiding the problem, it takes its finger off the fight-or-flight button and we feel relief. But, unfortunately, any anxiety we avoid in the present will be compounded in the future. Here's why. When we answer that call to action—*Woo-woo-woo! Do something!*—by acting on the perceived threat—treating it as a real problem—we are *confirming* that perception. Every time we confirm a perception of threat, we are in effect, giving a banana to the monkey mind. (Do you see why I love this metaphor?)

That's how the innocent little behaviors we do to control our stress, like worrying and checking and planning, wind up creating more stress. When we treat an unknown as a problem we must do something about, we reward our little security guard with a bonus, encouraging it to sound the alarm whenever this, or any similar unknown, appears again. We are caught in a cycle of anxiety that completes another turn every time we feed the monkey!

And oh, how that cycle turns! Since the monkey has its finger in everything we do, we are answering its calls to action dozens, even hundreds of times a day. Many of our monkey-feeding microbehaviors are so subtle and ubiquitous that we are completely unaware of them, just as we are unaware of the emotions that trigger them. This is how we stay trapped in a cycle of worry and stress, continuing to believe that we can only relax when we are certain there is no threat—or, in other words, not very often. The peace and ease we strive for will never manifest. When we believe that and behave as if safety is our only value, we serve the monkey. While the monkey makes a good servant, it makes a terrible master.

Chronic anxiety and worry are an exorbitant price to pay for survival. But we don't need to keep paying it indefinitely. If we can tolerate the fight-or-flight feelings, ignoring the monkey's call to action, we reject the perception of threat. The message we send is *I can handle not knowing.* The monkey gets no banana. This is how we interrupt and reverse the anxiety cycle. It's how we build confidence in our ability to cope with the unknown. And it's how we build a new mind-set that accepts the inevitable uncertainty of life. It's how we master the monkey.

I can almost hear you thinking, *Wait a minute, welcoming the idea of uncertainty sounded cool. But welcoming the feeling of uncertainty sounds overwhelming.*

You're right. Fight-or-flight feelings can easily overwhelm us. That's because we're using the wrong muscle to deal with them. In the next chapter, I'll show you the right muscle, and how to make it stronger.

Resilience

Every summer there is a county fair held in our town, with lots of food that's fun to eat, and rides that make you want to throw up. I always drag my husband to the fair, in no small part because of those rides. It's not that they are easy for me. When I strap myself into my seat on the Chair-O-Plane, I am so scared that I literally *Woo-woo-woo!* like a monkey. As the ride begins, then accelerates, my body is awash in fight-or-flight feelings that I instinctively want to resist. My hands grip the safety bar in a rigid row of white knuckles.

But my intention is not to merely survive the ride. At some point, as I hurtle through space, defying the laws of gravity, I relax my hands on the bar. I soften my shoulders. I open my chest. I surrender. I am helpless, undefended. And in the opening space I create, my terror is joined by my excitement. As I push past what feels safe, I am more alive. If you've ever ridden a ride at an amusement park, you know exactly what I'm talking about!

Each of the exercises in this book is like a ride at the fair. To get our money's worth, we can't white-knuckle our way through them. When we do, we reinforce our monkey mind's perception that the practice is dangerous and we're lucky to get out of it alive. Our resistance only strengthens the grip of anxiety and fear upon our lives.

When we do not resist the anxiety and fear that uncertainty brings, we are surprised to find that these emotions are not fatal. We can let go of our grip on the bar. We don't have to hold on tight to survive. We can be anxious, afraid, even terrified, but if we don't resist, if we don't contract, if we expand our breath and our hearts to make space for what's happening, we can feel the infinite capacity for life within us. This welcoming is how we awaken our superpower: resilience.

The Welcoming Muscle

When we think of having resilience to negative emotions, we think of it as our ability to resist them, to white-knuckle them into submission. When an uncertainty in our life arises, we literally tense certain muscles in our bodies. We try to get a grip on it and ride it out, like a scary ride at the amusement park. As a result, many of us find ourselves in a state of physical tension all of the time. What we don't understand is that resilience has nothing to do with resistance; in fact, it's just the opposite.

If you pay close attention to your body when you're feeling overwhelmed by negative emotions, you'll notice that there are certain muscles or groups of muscles that contract, trying to resist your emotions. For every resisting muscle that is repeatedly tense and overused, there is a corresponding muscle or muscle group that is stretched and underused. In order to build resilience to negative emotion, the tense muscle of resistance to the unknown must be relaxed so the opposing "welcoming muscle" can be exercised.

So where exactly is this welcoming muscle that will hold us open to the unknown? To get a feel for it, try this exercise. (You can download a guided audio version at http://www.monkey mindbooks.com/u.)

Think of something that has you worried or uncertain. With that thought in mind, imagine yourself on a roller coaster or any scary amusement park ride. Hunch over and tighten your hands on the safety bar until your knuckles are white. Hold your stomach tight, emptying your lungs and staying in that position for a moment without taking in any air. Notice what you are feeling. Then go ahead, inhale, and sit up as normal.

Now, imagine yourself back in the seat of that scary ride, gripping the bar and exhaling, but this time when you inhale and sit up, lift your arms above your head and stretch your body to its full height. If it's okay in your environment, let out a scream or a roar. Stay erect for a moment, squeezing your shoulder blades together and relaxing your belly. Imagine that same worry again in this new position. Notice what this feels like.

This exercise demonstrates in a physical way how our met-aphorical welcoming muscle works. In our contracted position, we feel tense, weak, and resistant to the unknown. In our expansive position, we feel open, strong, and welcoming. In the exercises in this book, welcoming fight-or-flight sensations will be like flexing unused muscles we didn't know we have. This will take practice; we'll take it slowly, feeling our way forward following a clear guideline at our own pace.

But don't kid yourself that it will protect you from discomfort. Like the Chair-O-Plane, discomfort is part of this ride. As the bodybuilders say, "No pain, no gain!" Or, as I tell my clients, "We cannot heal until we feel."

Sweating the Small Stuff

That's all well and good for some people, you might say, but *my* emotions are *too* overwhelming. When I get slammed at work, or have a pain in my chest, I can't help but worry. When I don't know where my mate or my child is, I simply *must* check. If I try to go through my day feeling my emotions without resisting them, I'll be a quivering mess, unable to function.

I understand your apprehension. I am a born worrier who has always been highly sensitive. I know firsthand what anxiety feels like, and as a mental health practitioner who has made a specialty of anxiety disorders, I've worked with hundreds of clients exhibiting every variety and intensity of negative emotion imaginable.

What I do in my clinical practice, and what I have endeavored to do in this workout, is create an empowering practice for developing resilience to the negative emotions that are keeping us anxious and worried. Following this practice faithfully will give you maximum support—before, during, and after the exercise. You'll have everything you'll need for success.

If, however, any exercise looks like it's too much for you, scale it down a little. Treat each exercise as a starting point and then adjust it to your own personal tolerance level. Riding the bumper cars might be what you can handle at first, and that's okay. Remember, each exercise should be a low-stakes situation where you can experience the discomfort of your negative emotions without getting overwhelmed and aborting your mission. By working within this sweet spot, I've proven again and again—both in my personal and professional life—that every emotion, positive *and* negative, has both a beginning and an end.

And neurological studies back me up. When we allow our sympathetic nervous system to fire without resisting it, two things happen: first, the fight-or-flight neurochemicals that are making us feel so worried and stressed, metabolize, and, second, the parasympathetic nervous system gets activated, unleashing rest-and-digest neurochemicals to replace them. This two-step procedure conditions the limbic system not to fire up so quickly the next time that situation arises. Ultimately, our resilience to uncertainty is directly proportionate to our resilience to negative emotion. Resilience is the only thing that tames the monkey mind.

So, what I am saying is Yes, *do* sweat the small stuff! Feel your heart pounding and your stomach tying itself into a knot. Experience each uncertainty in its fullness. Let the unknown remain unknown. Let the drama play out. Whatever emotion arises, breathe with it, unresisting from beginning to end. Only then can we possess the confidence that we can cope with whatever life may bring. It is confidence in our own resilience—not certainty that our situation is safe and predictable—that will enable us to relax when we want to, be flexible when we need to, spontaneous when we are inspired, and joyful simply for being alive.

The Workout

This workout is made up of thirty exercises, one month's worth of instruction. While a few of the exercises should be done in sequence, most of the exercises can be done in any order, and all can and should be repeated. You can, for example, do the same exercise two or more days in a row. If an exercise feels overwhelming, you can tweak it a little to make it manageable, or skip it altogether. If an exercise does not make you anxious at all, go on to another, or just do it for fun. And if it doesn't work for the day you have planned, you can always come back to it later. In short, there is no hard-and-fast rule about the sequencing of your personal program. Since the *I-must-be-certain* mind-set affects all your behavior in every situation, doing *any* exercise that undermines it will begin to change the way you experience *every* uncertainty that arises in your life.

So let's break down the exercise format. On the page preceding all but the first exercise, there will be a short story or cartoon, and a thought-provoking question. These are best read the day before you do the exercise as a way of warming to the situation to be addressed.

On the following page, you'll see the title and a short description of the exercise followed by a sequence of graphic icons representing each aspect of the exercise in more detail. Here's what they mean:

A brief explanation of the specific "monkey mind-set" that pertains to this exercise and the negative emotions we can expect to hijack us.

Description of the "welcoming muscles" we'll be working to build resilience to these negative emotions, and the new expansive mind-set that we will be redirecting ourselves toward.

The higher values and aspirations we will be supporting when we do this exercise.

A postexercise review in the form of questions to ask yourself. *Note:* A more extensive review for each exercise is offered in the form of downloadable worksheets, which you can find at http://www.monkeymindbooks.com/u.

These are essentially the same steps I coach my clients through in my office, but unlike my clients, you're doing these exercises alone. Much as I'd like to, I can't be your personal trainer. I can, however, provide you with some tools that will help you act as your own trainer. With these tools, you'll be well equipped to coach yourself through the exercises, just like a personal trainer in a gym would coach you through a physical exercise routine. That said, there is one essential ingredient that all effective personal trainers and therapists have that I can't squeeze into this book. That's a voice telling you, "You're doing great. Keep it up!" Much as I want to, I cannot give you on-the-spot positive feedback. To be successful in this program, you must be your own cheerleader. You're going to have to praise yourself.

Over the years in my clinical practice, I've experimented with different ways my clients could praise themselves while they are not in session with me. I've taught them to chart their success on a form like the downloadable forms I offer for this workout. I've encouraged them to use whimsical rewards like stars and stickers, or to even pat themselves on the back!

Silly as it sounds, patting oneself on the back *does* reinforce new behavior. It is a *kinesthetic* reinforcement, a physical ritual that reinforces the new behavior you just accomplished. Your own kinesthetic reinforcement can be any action you choose, moving a coin from one pocket to another, taking a deep breath, or mouthing the words "well done." My favorite is the *wristband switch*.

Everybody has a drawer with rubber bands—dig out a nice big one and slide it around your wrist. (If you have a stretchy beaded wristband or something similar, that's even better.) Every time you welcome a negative emotion and/or redirect yourself to your expansive mind-set, simply move the flexible band from one wrist to another.

Kinesthetic Reinforcement

Believe me, once you're wearing this powerful teaching tool, you'll see plenty of opportunities to use it. I wear one nearly every day, as do most of my clients, and there are days when I switch mine back and forth a dozen times. Time and time again, I've proven to myself that reinforcing new behavior helps master the monkey—which brings me to my final pitch.

Our Daily Sweat

As this book goes to press, it will be over two years since the fire, two years since I wondered whether I could ever feel confident and relaxed, not to mention joyful, again. I'm happy to tell you that I feel more relaxed, more confident, and, yes, more joyful than I've been at any time of my life. It's not because my home has been rebuilt and soon will be ready to move into, although I am deeply grateful for that. And it's not because these two years have been easy; there have been many challenges, including the coronavirus pandemic. But I was able to handle that imminent threat with more confidence and clarity than in the past. These strengths are a direct result of my exercising my welcoming muscle on a regular basis. I break a sweat every chance I get.

Why is it so important to have an exercise program in place, even for someone like me who understands anxiety inside and out? Because my future, like yours and everyone else's, is uncertain. When we find ourselves in unfamiliar situations where the outcome is beyond our control, we will be hammered with negative emotions. Unless we are prepared for these emotions, they will hijack us into a monkey mind-set, and we'll start to think and behave as if certainty is the only thing that matters. Since the monkey mind is so much louder and faster than we are, all this will happen before we are even aware of it.

The welcoming exercises in this workout are designed to heighten our awareness of the monkey's work, to help us learn to recognize when we are being hijacked so we can change our stance from resistance to welcoming. We're creating emotionally charged, mentally off balance experiences where we can learn to redirect ourselves to a healthy mind-set and build resilience. To handle the big stuff the future holds, we practice by sweating the small stuff. We want to make a regular habit of welcoming uncertainty. We need to get our daily sweat!

I hope you'll commit to this workout for a full thirty days. After you complete it, take the *Intolerance of Uncertainty Quiz* that I mentioned in the introduction one more time. (If you haven't already taken it, make sure you do so before you start the workout.) This quiz is the baseline you'll use to compare your tolerance for uncertainty before and after the four weeks of the workout. But if you give your all to the exercises, you won't need the quiz to be aware of a new level of confidence in your own resilience, nor to be aware of the higher aspirations that will manifest in your life. I'm confident that once you begin to experience the joys of being flexible, spontaneous, curious, creative, present, and at peace, you will want to make these exercises an important part of your daily routine—regularly flexing that welcoming muscle, mastering the monkey, and building the resilience you need to face an uncertain world, confident and relaxed!

But that's looking ahead. Now, it's time to get started. To get us up and running, the Day One exercise is a foundational exercise to help us get more in touch with the space where we'll be welcoming uncertainty—our bodies. It's an especially accessible exercise, something anybody can do—even *you* can do it no matter how apprehensive you are about the workout. Remember, the only bad exercise is the one that didn't happen. So, what are you waiting for? *Let the welcoming begin!*

Welcoming Warm-Up

Today, we are going to listen to a five-minute *Welcoming Uncertainty Practice* in which I will guide you through the processing of the negative emotions and uncomfortable sensations that accompany uncertainty. This foundational exercise is the most important in the workout. It's so crucial to your success that I have made a variation of it available for most of the exercises. Think of it as a warm-up, a stretching exercise to prepare you for what lies ahead. You can also use it as a backup for when you feel overwhelmed by any exercise. The more you practice with this recording, the better equipped you'll be to handle not only the exercises ahead but also any challenge that you face in your life!

As I said in the introductory chapters, we must not only be able to welcome uncertainty with our minds but also with our bodies. This can be especially difficult when we experience fight-or flight sensations like tightness in the chest, stomach, or throat, and negative emotions like fear and panic. Our mind-set is *Negative emotions mean something is wrong, I need to do something.* For the exercises in this book, we will forgo the usual ways we react to this discomfort—checking for reassurance or distracting ourselves, for example—and, therefore, we will feel them more acutely. Our instinct will be to tighten up our bodies or to "white-knuckle" our way through the exercise. This is only another way of resisting uncertainty, and, as such, it feeds the monkey, programming our limbic system to make us more anxious whenever we are faced with similar situations.

The audio recording *Welcoming Uncertainty Practice* guides us step-by-step with a powerful alternative to white-knuckling. It will help us learn to breathe into our discomfort, soften our body, and surrender to the feelings we've been resisting. When we welcome the emotions and sensations that arise with the unknown, we teach the monkey mind that uncertainty is not cause for alarm, and we condition ourselves to a new expansive mind-set: *Negative emotions are to be felt, not acted on. It is okay to feel this way.* And, as you will discover, when we don't resist uncomfortable sensations and emotions, they change all on their own!

With repetition, this exercise will lower blood pressure, reduce stress hormones, and decrease muscle tension. Over time, it will reduce worry, anxiety, and chronic stress. Ultimately, it will increase your ability to relax, to be present in this moment, to be at peace.

For those of you without internet access, here is the *Welcoming Uncertainty Practice* script.

Sitting or lying down, eyes open or closed, bring your attention to your breath. Notice the temperature of the air as you breathe in through your nose and the temperature as you breathe out. You may notice the air is cool as you inhale and warm as you exhale.

Now bring your attention to the top of your head. Move down to your eyes, your jaw, your throat, your neck and shoulders. Move down your arms to your hands. Notice if there is any tension, warmth, coolness, or tingling. Open the palms of your hands skyward, as a physical reminder that you are allowing yourself to feel whatever it is you are experiencing at this moment, whether pleasant, unpleasant, or neutral. Bring your attention to your chest and heart, your stomach, your hips and thighs, your calves and all the way down to your feet. Imagine that there is a welcome mat at your feet.

Bring your attention to any areas of your body where you feel discomfort. This could be physical pain like a headache or backache. You may notice uncomfortable sensations like tightness in your chest or a rapid heartbeat. If you are not feeling any discomfort, see if you can notice any neutral sensations. Bring your attention to your hands and notice any warmth, coolness, tingling, pulsing. Whatever you are feeling in your body, allow it to be just as it is. There is nothing you need to fix, change, or figure out. Tell yourself, *It is okay to feel just as I am feeling right now.* As worries or judgments appear, just notice them, gently reminding yourself that you do not need to figure anything out right now. Open up to how these thoughts make you feel—anxious, confused, overwhelmed—and breathe into this.

Bring your attention back to your breath again, noticing your inhalations and exhalations. Now imagine that you are breathing into any area of your body where you feel sensations. If there is pain, breathe into it. Use your breath to open to this feeling, to soften and surrender to it. If there is an uncomfortable sensation, breathe into it, making room and space for what is. Instead of tensing up, relax into the sensation. If you are not experiencing discomfort, breathe into your hands or feet, making room for warmth, coolness, tingling.

As you tune into your body and allow yourself to feel whatever you are feeling, you will notice a natural ebb and flow—sensations will at times intensify and at times subside. This is normal and natural, let this happen.

What sensations did you notice during this exercise? What emotions did you experience? Don't judge your success by how relaxed and present you felt during or afterward. The rewards of this practice are cumulative and take time to manifest. Congratulate yourself for your willingness to stop and turn your attention inward, regardless of what you may have found.

Most of us use our phones a lot, so often that we aren't conscious we're doing it. In our next exercise, we'll shine some light on this ubiquitous habit.

2

Count Your Check'ns

Every time we pick up our cell phones to check on something today, we will take notice and take count. Whether we are checking our email, social media, texts, or the weather, our mission is to monitor. To keep track, you can use the tally chart included with the *Personal Training Tools*, or keep count on a piece of paper or on your phone. Either way, you'll have a better awareness of your cell phone checking at the end of the day. This is of paramount importance because we cannot change what we are not aware of.

When we track our cell phone checking, we will begin to notice the urges that immediately precede checking as well as the subtle emotions that prompt these urges. These emotions are a limbic system warning that we may be missing out on something—either an opportunity, such as an invitation from someone, or a threat, such as the news of an accident. The monkey mind wants us to be informed all the time. Each urge that we act on by picking up our phone is evidence that our higher brain has been hijacked. We've adopted a mindset that says, *To be safe and productive, I must always be in the know.*

We can't break our cell phone habit in a day or in a month, nor is that our purpose today. Our job is to expand our self-awareness, to notice what we're feeling when we get the urge to reach for our phone. In addition to boredom, these feelings may include agitation or irritation, anxiety, fear, and desire. The mind-set we are cultivating is one of nonjudgment and compassion: *I can watch my own urge to check my phone with detachment and welcoming.*

You may not feel that observing feelings and behavior helps anything. It may even be distressing to know how often you check. But monitoring our cell phone use is a powerful first step toward changing the behavior that has kept us in the anxiety cycle. Every time you notice yourself checking your phone and add to your count, move your wristband (see The Workout) to acknowledge that you are doing a great job.

Questions to ask ourselves: How many times did I check my phone? What feelings or sensations did I notice? As I observed my checking behavior, did I do so with judgment or compassion?

Don't mistake this for an accounting exercise. This is a mindfulness exercise. The only purpose for counting our checking is that it helps us focus on the moments we feel the urge to check. If you lose count, or forget to count, no problem! Return to exercising your awareness and begin counting again.

Are you a serial cell phone checker? Tomorrow, we'll take a stab at bringing down the count.

Curb the Urge

3

Today, we will begin to exercise some control of our cell phone checking. Now that we are more aware of our phone-checking habit from yesterday's practice, we're ready to do something about it. Set a goal for the number of times you'll check it today, for instance 75 percent of yesterday's total. Then throughout the day, every fourth time an urge arises, opt not to check. An alternative strategy is to postpone checking for one to ten minutes every time you get the urge. You may discover that postponed urges disappear altogether. *Note that for the purposes of this exercise, answering calls and responding to texts, since they are initiated by others, need not count as checking behavior.*

Before smartphones, when we were standing in line at the grocery store and feeling bored or lonely, we might strike up a conversation with someone else in line. If we felt frustrated that we couldn't remember the star or director of a movie we'd had seen, we'd shrug and let it go. If we felt anxious about what was happening in the world, we waited patiently for the evening news.

Checking our smartphones confirms the monkey's perception that standing in line, forgetting movie trivia, and not knowing the latest news developments is a problem to solve. *Woo-woo-woo!* The relief we feel from checking is, at best, temporary, and every time we check, we feed that little critter, guaranteeing more limbic system alarms—and urges to check—in the future. We also feed this monkey mind-set: *Negative emotion is a sign something is wrong and I need to check my phone to feel better.*

Yesterday's exercise gave us a new awareness of our checking. We can begin to choose whether to feed the monkey or to feed the aspirations of our higher mind—resilience, confidence, peace, and presence in the moment. When we choose not to check, or postpone checking, we will feel withdrawal pain, but we will expand our minds and bodies to create a welcoming space for whatever we're feeling. Our new mind-set is *I can choose to experience this moment without checking my phone.* Reward yourself for redirecting yourself to this new mind-set by moving your wristband from one wrist to the other.

Every time we resist an urge to check our phones, we are taming the monkey mind, making it a little less twitchy and reactive, less prone to set off future limbic system alarms. Over time, we'll get fewer urges, and feel more relaxed and patient. Allowing difficult emotions to move through us without attempting to get rid of them with our phones, we become open to the present moment. This simple practice has powerful benefits!

⭐ Review questions to ask: Did I choose not to check on something with my phone even though I got the urge? Did I postpone checking? Did I open myself to the feelings and emotions that accompanied the urge? Did I redirect myself to an expansive mind-set?

Remember, if you reduced your total cell phone checking significantly today and hit your target, great. If you didn't, don't let that discourage you; numbers don't tell the whole story. If you offered a welcoming breath to your discomfort, and redirected yourself to your expansive mind-set *any* number of times, you are on the right track! You'll have plenty of opportunities to practice curbing your urges in the future!

Do you take a hypervigilant approach to health-related unknowns? Do you regularly check internet sites, friends and/ or health providers for assurance you are not sick? Tomorrow, we're going to try a healthier way to address health anxiety!

Lose Your Health Assurance 4

Today, we will refrain from seeking reassurance about our health. This includes calling or emailing our doctor, looking up symptoms on the internet, checking vital signs like pulse and blood pressure, feeling glands for swelling or forehead for fever, and examining urine or feces for color or consistency. (*Caveat:* If you are sick or have a medical emergency, postpone this exercise until you are healthy. If your doctor has you on a program that requires any these activities, like a daily blood pressure check for example, continue to follow your doctor's orders!)

Our bodies generate lots of sensations, many of them painful like indigestion, headache, or muscle pain. Other sensations, like tingling in our hands or feet or the feeling of our heart beating, though less painful, cause us anxiety just the same. The monkey mind doesn't like mystery and perceives these sensations as actionable. When it hits the anxiety button, we feel like we should do something. We think with the monkey's mind-set, which says, *To be safe, I need to monitor and control the sensations in my body.*

But research shows that prolonged stress and anxiety weaken our body's immune system. If we are relatively healthy, worrying about and checking on our health is more likely to make us sick than it is to keep us healthy. It also pulls us away from whatever is happening in the moment, hampering our ability to be productive, to relax, and to connect with others. How can we stop worrying and stressing about the mysterious spots, aches, and pains that we encounter all the time?

First, we must learn to make intelligent assessments of our body's random expressions, recognizing that most sensations are just noise that will soon quiet down and resolve themselves. The expansive mind-set we will adopt is *Unless it persists, an uncomfortable bodily sensation is not a signal that something is wrong.*

Second, we must behave in accordance with our assessment and mind-set. That means we will welcome the random expressions of our body, resisting the urge to do something about them. Every time we *don't* seek reassurance on a health-related unknown, even though it makes us feel more anxious now, we are programming our nervous system to relax and training the monkey mind to make us less anxious in the future. And to train yourself, move your wristband every time you welcome a bodily sensation without acting on it!

With repeated practice of this exercise, you will learn to trust your body more, allowing you to be confident, without the distraction of worry. A healthy state of mind is what best supports a healthy state of body!

☆ This exercise will challenge some of us a lot more than others. If you presently have a lot of health anxiety, don't judge yourself harshly for not being perfect. Give yourself credit for those urges you *did* resist. Even responding to a single urge by opening to the feelings that provoke it and redirecting yourself to your expansive mind-set is a step in the right direction!

I'm someone who likes to be on time for meetings, and I like that about myself. But the flip side of this preference for promptness is that if I think I am going to be even a minute late to something, I get anxious, stressed, and worried. This leads to chronic clock checking. After one morning commute, I calculated that I checked my dashboard clock an average of once a minute—twenty-five times during a twenty-five-minute drive. And I wasn't even running late that day! I knew something had to change.

The next day I got some duct tape and covered up my clock on the dash. I resolved that from that day forward I wouldn't check the time while I was driving. I didn't have to wait long to get a workout. On my first trip, it rained so hard that traffic slowed to 20 mph and it became pretty apparent I was going to be late. My eyes kept darting to the clock over and over, but, of course, it wasn't telling me anything. Let's just say that I was very uncomfortable for that trip. But I kept up with this exercise just the same.

One morning a month later, I was on my commute again when the traffic came to a standstill. A few minutes went by before I suddenly noticed that I was too busy listening to my music to think about being late. And instead of glancing at the clock, I was enjoying the beautiful Sonoma County skyline and the clouds floating by. I was so happy to discover something new to like about myself. I can handle the possibility of being late!

When you are driving, do you need to stay on schedule? Do you get stressed if bad weather, an accident on the road, or getting behind a slow driver threatens to make you late? Tomorrow, we'll tackle one of the behaviors that create that stress.

5   Pace, Don't Race

While we are commuting, running errands, or doing taxi service for the kids today, we won't consult the clock. You will set your own pace while on the road, remaining uncertain when you will arrive. This may require putting a piece of tape over the clock on your dash so you can't see it, and putting your cell phone out of easy reach so you aren't tempted to look. (If you don't drive, do the exercise whatever your method of transportation.)

To arrive on time, we take the reasonable step of leaving on time. But once we're on the road, getting stressed out over things we can't control—like traffic, other drivers, the weather, or road conditions—gets in the way of being relaxed and present in the moment. The microbehavior that contributes the most to this problem is our innocent little glance at the dashboard clock. Every time we check the time, we train our limbic system that being late is dangerous, and we replay the mantra of the monkey: *I can only relax if I know I will arrive on time.*

When we purposely choose not to know whether we're on schedule, our limbic system will remind us that we *should* know. We are likely to feel nervous about the consequences of our potential lateness, and the shame and/or disappointment that might entail. We may feel impatient, resenting every red light and slow driver in our path. This is the monkey mind throwing a tantrum. Instead of feeding the little beast by checking the clock, we'll breathe into our discomfort with welcoming acceptance. The message we send to our time-sensitive monkey mind—and the expansive mind-set we are building for ourselves—is *I can relax and be present in this moment without knowing if I'm on schedule or not.* And every time you send that message, along with using a welcoming breath, reward yourself by moving your wristband!

By welcoming the anxiety, fear, impatience, and shame that may arise with the possibility of arriving late, we build resilience to those emotions. With enough repetition, this practice will allow us to relax and enjoy the ride everywhere we go, confident that we can cope with walking into that meeting after it's already started!

Okay, let's evaluate how you did. If you covered your car clock and put your phone out of sight, good for you! How did it feel not to know the time? Did you welcome the feeling or did you white-knuckle the steering wheel? Did you remind yourself of your expansive mind-set and the values you were honoring? And if you arrived at your destination late because you couldn't check the time, great; there's no better way to grow our resilience than to get ourselves stretched a little.

Do you tend to eat the same thing for breakfast, shop for the same fruits and vegetables, and order the same food at restaurants? Ever wonder why, or what you're missing?

Take a Taste Test

Strawberry Jalapeño froyo, anyone? Today, we are going to hop out of our food rut by eating something that we have not eaten before. It could be a new frozen yogurt flavor like the hypothetical suggestion here, or if you have the courage, how about that scary vegetable you've been avoiding all your life?

It's easy to get into a rut with food. Eating what's familiar to us, what we like the taste of, is normal. It's also adaptable. If we went around popping any old thing into our mouths, we'd get sick! The monkey mind wants us to be certain that what we eat is safe and will make us thrive, and the surest way to do that is to eat what we ate yesterday. The monkey mind-set is *Sticking with foods that I know are good will keep me from feeling sick, disgusted, or disappointed.*

But with food, as with everything else, the cost of being certain is that it feeds the monkey, creating more anxiety—and less flexibility—about food in the long run. Needing to be certain that we will be satisfied by what we are going to eat contributes to our larger, system-wide *need-to-be-certain* about everything, which is neither adaptable nor fun.

Moving forward toward an unknown outcome—*Will I like it? Will I be disappointed? What if I waste my money on something I hate?*—and staying with the feeling that arises is our goal in this exercise. While it may seem inconsequential, when we successfully digest and metabolize our anxiety about what's on our plate, we enable a new way of thinking: *If I don't like this food, I can handle it, which frees me up to try new things.* This is a mind-set that will help us better tolerate uncertainty in every aspect of our lives. Reward yourself when you use this mind-set and welcome uncomfortable feelings by moving your wristband.

Trying new foods develops flexibility, keeping our life from getting stale and broadening our horizon. It creates new pathways in our brain, encouraging curiosity and creativity. And it can be fun!

⭐ What emotions did you digest along with your new food? What values were you going after? Were you invested in whether you liked it or not? Remember that this exercise is not meant to prove that we can like something we didn't think we'd like. Whether you wind up loving it, hating it, or are indifferent to it doesn't matter. Reward yourself for letting go of the familiar and embracing uncertainty.

I was training a psychology intern on how to treat OCD, explaining the relationship between the "O," which is the obsession or intrusive thought (for example, that a door handle is germy) to the "C," the compulsion (in this case, using one's sleeve to open the door). "To break this connection," I told her, "clients need to purposely trigger the obsession by approaching a germy door handle and, resisting the compulsion to protect themselves, grip the handle with their bare hands. When they do this over and over, allowing themselves to get anxious and not giving in to the compulsion, eventually the obsession, as well as the anxiety, fades."

My intern, who was listening intently and taking notes, stopped and with a self-conscious chuckle, confided that she probably had a little bit of OCD herself. "Whenever I fly anywhere, as I enter the plane, I tap three times on outside of the plane to keep it from crashing."

"I get it," I assured her. "When the plane doesn't crash, it reinforces your superstition."

Then I asked her if she would be willing, next time she flew, to resist the compulsion to tap on the plane. "No way," she answered. "The stakes are too high!"

Do you, like most of us, have little rituals you do to keep something bad from happening, like knocking on wood after making a confident statement so as not to tempt the fates to prove you wrong? Do these habits help or hinder you to cope with an uncertain world?

Step on a Crack

Today, we will resist the urge to engage in a superstitious behavior. While you may not think of yourself as superstitious, the truth is most of us have subtle irrational habits we are completely unaware of. Does your good-bye to your loved ones include a default reminder to "drive safely"? Are certain days or dates "bad days" for making a big purchase or traveling? Perhaps you have a "lucky" piece of clothing or accessory to wear for special events or have a crystal hanging from your rearview mirror. Whatever your personal superstition, challenge it today. If you can't think of any, step on some cracks, find a black cat and let it cross your path, or walk under a ladder and notice whether doing these things make you feel uneasy.

When a departing loved one walks out our front door, since we can't be 100 percent certain they will return, our autonomic nervous system begins to deliver fight-or-flight alarms. Reminding them to "drive safely" makes those feelings go away temporarily, but it feeds the monkey and reaffirms the *must-be-certain* mind-set that *Life is dangerous and I must do something to decrease the risk.*

As our loved one leaves, or as we get on the plane, or whatever situation we exercise with today, we will welcome the fear that arises with open arms. We will not remind anyone to drive safely or knock on wood or the side of the plane. Since the future in these situations is not within our control, there is nothing to be done other than to allow the fear to dissipate on its own. And it always does. And as it dissipates, we will affirm our new expansive mind-set: *I can let go of what is beyond my control.* Reward that affirmation and the welcoming of fear by patting yourself on the back or by moving your wristband.

Dropping superstitious behaviors helps build resilience to negative emotions and trust in our ability to cope with the unknown. Freed from the impulse to act when there is nothing to be done, we will be better able to be relaxed and confident in future situations that are beyond our control.

What expansive mind-set did you practice while dropping a behavior? What emotions did you process? Remember that the purpose of this exercise is not to disprove superstitions, but to demonstrate that dropping superstitious behavior helps us process, and ultimately reduce, our fear of the unknown.

Does your need to know take precedence over what's happening in the moment? What would happen if we allowed some little mysteries to remain unsolved?

Can't Remember?
Let It Be

Every time we notice that we've forgotten something today, unless it's important, we will not try to remember it, ask anybody about it, or look it up. Whether we are trying to remember the name of a movie or actor, what year it was we took that vacation to Hawaii, what kind of a bird makes that call, what we walked into the garage to get, or the name of the fictional city that Batman calls home, today we are going to give our brains and phones a break, not because there is anything wrong with trying to remember trivial things, but because it's a good uncertainty exercise. And, of course, we'll continue to unleash our powers of recall for those *non*trivial pursuits, like the location of our car keys and the four-digit code to our debit card!

When we remember our keys and passwords, things run more efficiently. When we remember what to pick up at the grocery store, we don't have to make a second trip. And when we remember the names of the people in our lives, we are building stronger relationships. But the monkey mind has trouble differentiating between what we need to remember to survive and thrive and what we just want to remember. Our need to know is baked in. Forgetting something that is inconsequential can trigger uncertainty just like forgetting something important does, sparking a sense of urgency. When we act as if something inconsequential *is* urgent to know, by focusing on trying to recall, asking someone about it, or looking it up, we feed the monkey and reinforce the mind-set that *I can only relax when I can remember everything.* This, of course, means we'll never be able to fully relax.

When we choose to allow things to remain forgotten today, defying our sense of urgency, we'll likely notice a wide range of uncomfortable emotions. We might experience simple confusion (*Wait! Hold on, I know that!*), frustration (*Why can't I remember this simple thing?*), loss (*But I really want to know that!*), or even panic (*Am I becoming senile?*). Or we might just feel deprived because looking things up can be fun and it can be gratifying to remember! Our job is to allow whatever feelings arise to wash over us, and to remind ourselves of our new, expansive mind-set: *I don't need to know this. I can let go.*

While today's exercise focuses on low-stakes memory gaps, it nevertheless builds our welcoming muscle and supports the higher values we aspire to, such as being present in the moment, for example. The better able we are to master our impulse to fill in the blanks of our past, the better we can relax into what's happening with us now.

Letting what is temporarily forgotten remain forgotten is also an exercise in trust, both in our own resilience and in our ability to recall what is truly important. When we stop fishing for a memory, we are often surprised to find it floating up to the surface on its own.

And finally, when we allow ourselves to feel the small loss of something we think we should remember, we are practicing self-compassion, which is great preparation for the inevitable moments when, as we grow older, memories become permanently lost.

⭐ Rewarding yourself for not knowing the answer may take some getting used to; after all, we've been taught the opposite since grade school. Just ask yourself, *What values did I choose by not indulging my need to know?* Give yourself a pat on the back for every time your memory failed and you succeeded at letting it fail. And if you can't remember all the times you chose not to try to remember something today, and you choose *not* to try to remember all of them, great! Double points for that!

Is your daily transportation routine set in stone? Are efficiency and predictability the only values that apply to your departures and arrivals? Tomorrow, we're going on a mini-expedition to the unknown!

9 Take the Road Less Traveled

Today, we are going to break from our normal route to work, to the gym, to daycare, or wherever we plan to go, and take an alternate route. You might google-map a new way to get there, or simply take a "wrong" turn and find your way by trial and error. You might use public transportation instead of driving, take Lyft or a taxi, hop on a bike, or just plain hoof it. Whichever way we choose to tweak our travel, the emphasis will be on the *going* there, not on the *getting* there.

There is nothing wrong with taking the most efficient and easiest transportation, but continually using the path of most certainty trains our limbic system that certainty is all that matters. We feed the monkey mind-set that *It is dangerous to waste time or be late. Any way other than the most efficient way is just plain silly!*

As commuters, we pay little attention to the experience of travel, arriving at our destination without any real memory of how we got there. And because we are rarely surprised by anything on our predictable trip, we are ill-equipped to deal with surprises. When our car breaks down or our train is late or the traffic stops, we are overwhelmed. We don't know how to be flexible and creative, or how to find another way. When our default path is our only path, we lose our ability to be present in the moment, we train ourselves to be rigid, and we cultivate a way of thinking that doesn't prepare us for the unexpected.

When we alter our travel routine, we will have thoughts telling us we are making a mistake. Rather than engaging with these thoughts, we will focus on reminding ourselves of our new expansive mind-set: *Travel is not simply something I want to get through, but also something I want to experience to the fullest, regardless whether it is easy, efficient, or reliable.* A new route is one way to get the full experience. With that experience, of course, will come negative emotions. We are likely to feel afraid that we are going the wrong way and may not arrive on time, feel impatient with the traffic or other obstacles we are unfamiliar with, feel foolish for choosing such an indirect route, or all of the above. These feelings are what we're after! Our job is to welcome them and allow them to be, and when you do, don't forget to give yourself some praise!

By taking the road less traveled, we'll see new sights, hear new sounds, awaken our senses, and get a slightly different perspective on life, all without spending any extra money or taking time off work! And more important, we are training ourselves to be more flexible, creative, and present in the moment.

Hopefully you didn't wind up hopelessly lost or horribly late, but if you did, that's okay, because a smooth trip is not what you are after with this exercise. Here are the questions to ask yourself: What expansive mind-set did you use? What emotions did you embrace? What values did you cultivate? If you can answer those questions, you nailed it!

In every neighborhood I've ever lived in, there has been one house with an unnaturally pristine garage. Except for a box or two, maybe a broom leaning in the corner, and perhaps a couple bikes, there would be nothing but bare walls and endless floor space. In contrast, my own garage was crowded with floor-to-ceiling stacks of cardboard boxes overflowing with old clothes, camping equipment, tools, and remnants of my grown children's "treasured" belongings. Any single piece of the clutter, when held in my hand, represented a possibility. Might I need this leftover pipe insulation someday? What if my son wants to reminisce over his drawings from second grade? If I have this rocking chair reupholstered it might be nice in my office. After several of these impasses I would leave decluttering to another day. But deep in my soul I knew that someday, somehow, I would have a garage like my neighbor's.

When my home burned down to the ground in the California wildfires of 2017, all my clutter as well as all the treasures were gone. This is not how I imagined I would get a pristine garage. I was totally unprepared for such a massive loss. This experience, while heartbreaking, taught me that all the things that I thought I could not do without, could either be done without or replaced. And I discovered that the pain of loss could not only be endured but would expand my ability to appreciate the new material things that came my way, things that I don't need to hold on to so hard.

Are you all too familiar with the feeling of holding on to things like clothes, furniture, or other mementos of the past? Tomorrow, we'll get a taste of the pain—and the joy—of letting go.

Decide to Declutter

Today, we are going to throw away or give away something we no longer use. It could be clothing you have not worn in ages, something boxed up in your garage, or the odds- and-ends junk in that kitchen drawer. Set your timer for five minutes because that is all the time allowed to decide what you will get rid of.

Most of us have a lot of stuff, and there is a good reason for this. To live in this world, we need food to keep us nourished, clothes to keep us warm, tools to build and repair things, furniture and art to give us comfort and pleasure. From the beginning of time, humans have collected, bartered, and traded with an eye toward possessing *more*. Securing more stuff and holding on to the stuff we have is central to our survival. But while we have evolved, our monkey mind has not, and it cannot discern when enough is enough. To the monkey, *It's dangerous to let go of anything you might need in the future.*

If we choose whether to buy, sell, or hold by following the prompts of our limbic system, we end up with too much stuff. The more we collect and protect the material things we "might need someday," the more we train the monkey that we cannot survive without them. This cycle leads to an overall state of insecurity and possessiveness. Lacking the experience of small material losses, we never learn how to cope with them. This leaves us unprepared for the bigger losses—like the loss of health and loved ones—that are in store for us no matter how much we accumulate.

Today, we're going to deliberately expose ourselves to a new uncertainty by letting go of something we might need in the future. We will practice tolerating the feeling of loss, breathing it in, allowing it to pass through us without acting on it. When we surrender to loss, it cannot hold us hostage anymore. And by doing so, we will reinforce a more expansive mind-set: *When I let go of something, it strengthens my ability to cope with loss.* When you let go, feel the loss, and think in this new way, move your wristband to a different wrist to acknowledge your hard work!

As we grow more resilient to the fear of loss, we learn to trust in our own resourcefulness should we ever miss what we've given up. We gain confidence that we can cope with an uncertain future, trusting ourselves to find a creative solution to whatever the situation requires. And as we decrease the clutter in our lives, we create free space for more happiness and joy. In the words of Thich Nhat Hanh, "Letting go gives us freedom, and freedom is the only condition for happiness. If, in our heart, we still cling to anything—anger, anxiety, or possessions—we cannot be free."

⭐ It is easy to be distracted by whether your choice(s) of what to get rid of was wise or not. This exercise is not about the relative usefulness of things, but rather our emotional relationship to things. What emotions did you feel during this exercise? If you felt the pain of loss long enough for it to dissipate on its own, you did it right!

Are you a clock checker? Do you worry about arriving later than you planned to or were expected to? Would you like to be more open, relaxed, and present in the moment, even if you are uncertain if you are running on schedule?

Get Off the Clock

Pick an hour of your day today during which you will not check the time. It could be your lunch hour or any sixty-minute period of the day where knowing the exact time is not essential for your job or well-being. This time blackout means you don't check your cell phone or computer clocks, your car clock, or wall clocks at work or home. It is fine to set a timer for the period you will be off the clock so that you know when your practice is over.

Does an hour without a clock check sound too challenging? Then do it for thirty minutes. Or if an hour seems too easy for you, try it for the whole morning or afternoon. Wherever your need-to-know pain threshold is, that's where you want to be working that welcoming muscle.

When we choose not to check the clock, we can expect to feel uneasy. To the monkey mind, not knowing whether we are on schedule is dangerous. We're going to be anxious that we are falling behind and don't have time to finish what we're doing. We'll feel afraid that we might be late for our next obligation. If we are relaxing and off the clock, we may feel guilty and question whether we are acting responsibly. We are also likely to feel impatient, wanting the allotted hour to be up so we can return to our regularly scheduled program! All these emotions will prompt a strong urge to check the time.

But as we have learned, the act of checking the clock confirms the mind-set that *I must be certain that I am on schedule or else I cannot relax.* The more we check the clock, the more we feel the urge to check. With our attention on the time, we can't fully experience what we're seeing, hearing, and feeling in the moment.

To get the full benefits of this exercise, we will welcome the fight-or-flight sensations that tell us to check, doing nothing in response except breathe. Instead of resisting these negative emotions, we'll open space in our bodies around them and give them plenty of room to play themselves out. To facilitate this process, we'll engage our new expansive mind-set: *I can learn to relax without knowing I am on schedule.* And don't forget to move your wristband and praise yourself when you resist the urge, remind yourself of your expansive mind-set, and breathe into the emotions and sensations in your body!

With enough off-the-clock practice, the agenda-driven monkey mind can be tamed. Without our unconscious need to adhere to a schedule, we can be more flexible, spontaneous, and creative. Going off the clock frees us to be present, and no matter what time it is, the present moment is all we have.

☆ What emotions did you encounter while off the clock? What values were you after? Remember, what makes this a successful workout is not whether you stayed on schedule despite not knowing the time. Our goal is to welcome the feeling of uncertainty about whether we're on schedule and to embrace our new mind-set that it's okay not to know. And if this exercise makes you late for something or you fall behind on your work, then you get an opportunity to practice coping skills—self-compassion and acceptance—that we all need with a future that is uncertain.

Other than email and text messages, the application I check most on my phone is my weather app. When planning trips, I've been known to begin checking the weather for my destination weeks ahead of time. At some point, I started checking the weather in my own town, and pretty soon I wouldn't go outside without first checking the air temperature! I decided this had to stop, so I assigned myself an exercise.

My husband, Doug, and I are fortunate to live near the ocean, and our favorite date is a long walk with the dog where the surf meets the sand, with a sunset car picnic afterward. Since the beach is often windy, as much as 20 mph, and the temperature can be twenty degrees colder than in town, it's sensible to check the weather before going. So naturally I did—multiple times throughout the day! What would happen if I didn't check at all?

The next beach date we had, every time I had the urge to check the weather during the day, and there were plenty of urges, I took a nice welcoming breath and moved my bracelet from one wrist to the other, telling myself what a good job I was doing and reminding myself of my expansive mind-set: It is more important to live life fully in the present moment than to predict what the weather will be like. I can cope regardless.

When the time came to leave, we packed extra clothes to be ready for any condition. On the drive out, I felt a little giddy with this date with the unknown. Doug and I made bets about how windy and cold it would be. I noticed myself looking at the trees more often as we got closer, *in order to see how much they were swaying, which was quite a lot, as it turned out. When we pulled up to our familiar spot the wind was blowing so hard I could barely open the door! But I felt great. I'd done the exercise and I was going to enjoy a bracing windy walk on the beach!*

What do you check most often—the news, the stock market, Twitter, or the weather? Or maybe all of the above?

12 Don't Feed on News Feeds

We're all used to getting a steady flow of news. Today, we'll turn off the spigot. Whatever your need-to-know area is—politics, finance, sports, or the weather—today you'll be uncertain. For how long is up to you. Some folks are so locked into their feeds that an hour will seem like too long. Others may want to cut loose for a whole morning or afternoon. Your goal is to find your own personal edge of discomfort and stay there for a while.

For most of human history, there was no such thing as too much information. When we lived in tribal villages, news came by word of mouth and the information was usually relevant and actionable—where the best fishing was, a storm was approaching, or someone was ill and needed assistance.

By contrast, modern news networks provide us with far more than we need to know. A report of a shark attack on other side of the world isn't relevant for or actionable by us, but thanks to the hyperreactivity of our limbic system, we are easily hijacked into becoming too frightened to go in the ocean. Whenever we hear about a tsunami, terrorist attack, stock market dip, or a rare virus anywhere in the world, we feel as though we need to do something about it. Usually the only thing we can do is to keep checking our news feeds to make sure the threat isn't getting bigger or closer. Our constant monitoring of the world at large keeps us distracted and disconnected from our immediate environment, which ironically, makes us less able to take care of ourselves.

Every time we check our news feeds, we program ourselves to fix the "problem" of uncertainty. The mind-set this cycle creates is *What I don't know will leave me unprepared and vulnerable to harm.*

To halt this cycle, we need to fully experience the negative emotion that arises when we have the urge to check our news feeds. That negative emotion may be the boredom we feel while riding an elevator or a worry that pops into our head while we're walking in the park.

When we resist the urge to distract or reassure ourselves by checking, we stay in the present moment and experience what we need to feel. The emotion will pass, and we will be that much more resilient—and that much more present—when we welcome it. We will be feeding a new mind-set: *It is more important to live life fully in the present moment than to anticipate possible threat.* And don't forget to move your wristband and praise yourself when you resist the urge, remind yourself of your expansive mind-set, and breathe into the emotions and sensations in your body!

This exercise will give you more time and energy to engage with the here-and-now events of the day. It will likely reduce your stress, lower your blood pressure, and it can even improve your sleep, especially if you restrict news feeds for several hours before you retire. And ultimately, becoming comfortable with not knowing whether all the news is good will make you more confident you can handle the bad news that eventually will arrive.

While doing this exercise, did you miss something you'd normally think of as important, or was it a slow news day? Neither outcome is relevant to your self-evaluation. What matters are your answers to the following questions: What emotions did I welcome? What expansive mind-set did I adopt? What values did I aspire to?

Do you feel bored and/or vulnerable without your cell phone?
If so, this is a great practice for you!

13

Go Without a Net

When we go out today, we will leave our phone behind. We will be unarmed, unencumbered, just as we were for thousands of years before the cell phone was invented. You may leave yours in your desk drawer when you go to meet colleague for lunch, or leave it on the kitchen counter when you go for a walk or to the grocery store. The length of time and situation to be endured in this vulnerable state are up to you.

 If we were walking a high wire a hundred feet above the earth, we'd need a safety net. If we were navigating in a strange city at night, we'd need a cell phone. But most of us treat our cell phones like a safety net, something we need to take *everywhere*, as if life itself were a high-wire balancing act. When we are without it, we are inundated with uncertainty and negative emotions.

These emotions range from worried (*What if my colleague can't find the restaurant and can't reach me?*) to fear (*What if there is an accident or health emergency and I need to call 911?*). We may feel frustrated (*I'm at the grocery store I can't call home to find out if we need eggs.*), bored (*What will I do in the doctor's waiting room?*), or just plain confused (*I'm lost! How do I get back?*). And that's just the short list!

Every time we go out the door with our virtual safety net, we train our brain—the primitive, reactive part of our brain, that is—to think the world is dangerous. The monkey mind, armed with the autonomic nervous system, trains us to bring our safety net everywhere we go by making us evermore uncomfortable when we're without it. Our mind-set is *Bad things can happen at any time, and I must have my cell phone to prevent a catastrophe.*

When the kinds of thoughts and emotions I listed above begin to flow, we will thank the monkey for its concern, take a welcoming breath, and turn to our new expansive mindset: *I can be more fully present and reasonably safe without my cell phone.* This trains our nervous system to calm down and teaches us that the world is not so dangerous that we always need to have a safety net. Whatever inconvenience arises, we can handle it. And every time you take that welcoming breath and redirect your mind-set, give yourself a little praise by moving your wristband!

With repetition, this exercise will enable us to feel more confident in our ability to manage situations like missed connections for lunch. We will become more flexible about getting the exact things we might need at the market. When boredom strikes in the waiting room, we'll get curious and creative. When we get lost, we'll get resourceful. And should we be in an emergency situation, whether we have a phone at or not, we'll be more focused and confident.

★ Review the negative emotions that came up while going without a net. Did you exercise your expansive mindset? If so, give yourself a pat or two on the back! If you didn't miss your phone that much, try going longer tomorrow. If you struggled, make it shorter next time. We want to find a balance where we're learning to cope without being overwhelmed.

I once treated a client who came to see me for insomnia. When I questioned her about what might be keeping her awake, she told me that she lived alone and didn't feel safe at night. Every time she closed her eyes, she imagined an intruder breaking in.

My client wasn't in any real danger. She'd lived in her upscale community with a state-of-the-art home security system for years without any incidents. Nevertheless, she'd recently enrolled in a neighborhood alert program that notified her in real time of any crime occurring within a five-mile radius of her home. She thought this extra layer of protection would make her feel more secure. Whenever she got a notice of a nearby incident of some kind, she would double-check her home security system "just to make sure." I'm no Sherlock Holmes, but it didn't take much sleuthing to solve the mystery of what was keeping her awake!

Do you need to hear your car beep to trust that you locked it? Do you retrace your steps to double-check that you turned the stove off or turned on the home alarm? What if you could trust that once is enough?

14

Don't Double-Check

When it comes to checking on things today, once will be enough. We won't double- or triple-check! By "double-check," I am referring to any security step that is *redundant*. When locking the car, for example, we won't press the key remote a second time to hear the car beep. When leaving home or office, we won't go back to make sure we locked up. Nor will we monitor our security cameras remotely for intruders. When we finish using the stove, curling iron, heater, or lights, we will turn them off or unplug them without reconfirming afterward that we remembered to.

Technology has made checking on our cars, homes, and even family members so easy that it's helped turn many of us into regular double checkers, unable to feel secure without an extra audible or visual confirmation that what is ours is safe. This seemingly innocent impulse to "make sure" is a reaction to uncomfortable feelings triggered from deep in our unconscious, in the lair of the monkey mind, which perceives news events—fires, thefts, kidnappings, and so on—as actionable threats. To this primitive part of our brain, the more a possible outcome is related to our safety, the more likely it is to occur. But what makes these incidents newsworthy is that they are rare. Every time we double-check, we feed that critter, guaranteeing more discomfort in the future and programing us to think we cannot trust ourselves or the world in general. We think, *The world is dangerous and I'm unreliable, so I better check again!*

When we resist our impulse to double-check, we welcome fear of the unknown. We'll imagine the worst scenarios—having our car broken into, our home invaded, appliances causing a fire—and feel pain of loss. As we breathe and relax around this discomfort, we give it space to dissipate, training the monkey mind that a second or third confirmation of safety is neither necessary nor helpful. Instead of reinforcing our need to know, we are growing our tolerance of uncertainty and a new expansive mind-set: *By taking reasonable precaution, I can trust myself and the world we live in.* Every time you review this mind-set and/or resist the urge to double-check, give yourself a little reward: move your wristband!

When we stop pursuit of the false confidence that double- and triple-checking offers, we discover the authentic confidence that allows us to truly relax, and that enables our spontaneity and joy to bloom. (Once my client stopped checking her home security system and disenrolled in the neighborhood alert system, she began sleeping through the night, and her days became more lively and productive.)

☆ It is likely you'll discover there was no need to double-check what you were uncertain about, and this is a valuable insight. But the purpose of this exercise is not to prove that double-checking is unnecessary. Our goal today is to focus on how many times you resisted the urge to double-check, not by white-knuckling but by opening to the uncertainty of what might happen. This is how we retrain the monkey mind.

At the supermarket, do you scan the checkout lines for the shortest queue with the precision and efficiency of a hawk hunting its prey? Do you get impatient when you're stuck in a line that's not moving? Tomorrow, we'll line up with a new intention.

15 Choose a Random Queue

Whenever we have an opportunity to choose between different lines of people today, we are going to choose a random line. Rather than choosing the most efficient route, leave it to chance. Decide ahead of time, for example, to queue up at the second line from the right, *no matter what.*

(*Note:* If you don't expect to go to a supermarket or pass through a bridge toll station or airport security today, save this exercise for another day when you expect to.)

By failing to take the quickest route forward, we'll provoke the monkey, and this will bring up an assortment of negative thoughts and emotions. We may have anxiety that we may be late—*This is taking forever!* We may feel jealousy that others are getting ahead of us—*I was here way before she was!* We'll probably get a dose of irritation—*They really should have more cashiers here!* We might feel even feel claustrophobic—*I'm trapped! Let me out of this line!* Or we might just feel bored out of our minds.

Indulging these thoughts or trying to squash our emotion by getting in a shorter or quicker line just reinforces the monkey mind-set at the root of all our discomfort: *If I don't choose the fastest line, I am wasting time and losing control of my day!*

Rather than contracting around our certainty-based thoughts and emotions, we will expand our hearts and minds to make room for them. If you are afraid you may be late to wherever you are going next, don't check the time. Surrender to that possibility and the feeling of falling behind schedule. If you feel bored waiting, resist the urge to check text messages and allow boredom to wash over you. And if, just as you unload your items on the conveyor belt, a new checker appears at the next counter and calls out, "I can take the next person in line," and the person *behind* you gets in that line and is done before your transaction has even started, great! Feel the clenching in your chest and hands and throw out that welcome mat! Remind yourself that *I can live life more fully in this present moment when I'm not trying to optimize it!* And remember to move your wristband and praise yourself!

Although this may look like an inconsequential practice, the expansive mind-set we are building with it will apply to hundreds of situations other than getting in lines. It will bring us more patience, openness, and a sense of peace in our lives. By opening to feelings of not being in control, we are training our fight-flight nervous system not to misfire and release unnecessary cortisol, which causes us physical and emotional stress.

The more negative emotions that this practice brings, the greater the indication that it is a great practice for you to repeat. It suggests that you are easily stressed when things get in the way of going to from point A to B. Most of our time spent is on our journey, not the destination, so learning to be more relaxed on our journey, has the most potential to bring happiness in our life.

⭐ Depending on the line you randomly choose, your experience of this exercise may vary greatly. Should you happen to randomly pick the shortest line, don't buy into your monkey's little happy dance, thinking, *This exercise is not as bad as I thought.* Getting through the queue quickly is not how you win this game. Do your own little happy dance celebrating that you left things up to chance.

My client Trish had recently moved and was using Facebook to stay connected with her old friends. What started out as an innocent way to deal with her loneliness had become a compulsion. She knew she was spending too much time on social media, and it was getting in the way of getting things done and developing roots in her new community.

My first assignment for her was to begin monitoring her Facebook activity. I asked her to keep track each day of everything she'd done the previous day on Facebook—making posts, tracking likes, reading feeds, everything.

Then she was to report back to me what she noticed.

When Trish came in to see me the next week, she'd made an important discovery. In the photos she was posting of herself, she was posing as happy and sexy. It was the only way she could be certain she'd get lots of likes and comments, which she checked on every two or three minutes after each posting. But no matter how many likes and comments there were, they didn't feel satisfying. And she felt uncomfortable looking at herself posing in her photos.

In her new life in a new town without her old friends, Trish was looking for reassurance that she was recognized and appreciated. But the recognition and appreciation she was getting for her Facebook posts were not based on her authentic self, but on what she thought was the only version *of herself that was certain to get her the attention and recognition she needed.*

Trish's assignment the following week was to limit herself to one post a day, based on the real Trish—the Trish who was willing not to know whether others would like and follow her—and to wait an hour before checking for likes and comments. And this would give her lots more time to devote to introducing the real Trish to her new city.

Do you spend more time on social media than you suspect is good for you? Wonder why Facebook, Instagram, and Reddit are so compelling? Tomorrow, we'll examine how we get hooked and what unhooking for a while can do for us.

Go on a Social Media Diet

16

Today, we're putting ourselves on a strict social media diet. That's right, no big Facebook feedings. No gorging on Instagram. Instead of snacking on posts, likes, and tweets whenever we get the urge, we'll limit ourselves to one scheduled meal of no more than thirty minutes' duration. That means planning a specific time to start and setting a timer to tell us when to stop. *Note:* To pull this off, we'll need to go to our settings and turn off all our social media alerts!

Facebook and other social media platforms are like crack to the monkey mind. The monkey mind perceives that every post, every tag, every tweet is potentially a threat or an opportunity requiring action. We are inundated with alarms, one after another crying, *Woo-woo-woo! Do something to make certain everything's okay!* The path to certainty is liking more posts, writing more tweets, and tagging more photos to solidify our relationships. All of these opportunities to check make our limbic system highly reactive, and that means more anxiety, worry, and stress for us. We are hijacked by this monkey mind-set: *If I don't know what's happening on social media, I'll be missing out.*

When we purposely stop logging on to social media, even for a short time, we activate uncertainty, doubt, and the unknown and may feel lost, lonely, bored, and afraid. This is not only to be expected, but it is also to be welcomed. When we open ourselves to this discomfort with our breath, with our whole bodies, we signal to the monkey mind that it's okay, we can survive without knowing what's happening in that space. We're strengthening an expansive mind-set: *By resisting the impulse to check social media, I am cultivating more calm and peace in my life.*

Remember to reward yourself as often as possible while you're logged off. Move your wristband every time you welcome emotion and redirect your mind!

Much of our social media activity is driven by our search for approval and recognition from others, but if we are so preoccupied with that search that we miss out on what's happening in the present moment around us, no amount of external validation will be enough. This diet exercise will put us exactly where we need to be to experience the higher values what will best sustain us: peace and presence in the moment.

While we must resist the social media urge, we mustn't white-knuckle it. We evaluate our effort by how well we *relaxed into* our fear of missing out and redirected ourselves to our expansive mind-set.

Do you have a problem that you just can't stop worrying about?
Tomorrow, we'll take a shot at a different kind of solution.

17

If This, Then That

Today, we will interrupt a worry cycle. Think of an uncertainty in your life that troubles you. For example, *My company is merging with another. I could lose my job.*

1. Ask yourself, *If I lose my job, then what?*

2. Answer the question with *action(s)* you could take. Examples: *I could reach out to family and friends,* and/or *I could get retraining,* and/or *I could read books about personal loss.*

When worry presents itself with big unanswerable questions that go around and around in our minds, it is a sure sign we've been hijacked. Not only are we *not* solving the problem, we're losing sleep as well as losing our concentration and our general sense of well-being. Worrying is a behavior that feeds the monkey, training it that any outcome we can't be sure about is a threat, and that if we could just eliminate the uncertainty (or get rid of the problem), we would be safe. And we are training ourselves to believe that *If I can't handle this problem, my life is ruined.*

When we reframe our worry as a question with an *actionable* answer, we (1) override the fight-or-flight signals to do something, and (2) reengage our higher brain. Then we engage it further by answering the question with hypothetical actions we could take.

Will our actionable answers bring us certainty about the outcome? No, but that's not what we're after. We want to stop obsessing about *what if* and be present with *what is*. This is how we learn that, while we can never be certain about anything, we can always be resourceful, creative, and resilient. It is how we build a better mind-set: *I can't solve every problem perfectly, but I can respond with resilience and wisdom to any problem that arises.* Every time you review this mind-set or interrupt worry with an actionable answer to a problem, move your wristband.

Every time we disrupt the worry cycle—in this case with an actionable plan—we program ourselves to experience less worry in future. We learn to trust that whatever happens, we can cope. This is how we gain the confidence we need to live fully in the present.

Remember that the "then that" you come up with is not intended to prevent "if this" from happening. Your purpose, and what you give yourself stars for, is to create a wiser response to the unknown than worrying.

A few years ago, my husband, Doug, and I took a trip to Costa Rica. I'd never been to Central America before so, while I was excited, I was also a little wary because of not knowing what to expect. To be on the safe side, I packed everything I thought I might need—clothes for different temperatures, all my favorite personal items like shampoo, lotion, sunscreen, and, of course, my cosmetics! I even threw in some first aid supplies. I felt pretty prepared for my first journey to what I thought of as a Third World country.

We arrived after midnight on New Year's Day to a nearly deserted airport. As we waited at the baggage claim, watching the other passengers pick up their luggage, it got quieter and quieter. Finally, it became evident that our luggage did not make the flight with us. My heart sank.

At the baggage claim office, we were told that our luggage would arrive within two days—hardly very reassuring to me. I panicked! There I was in this strange new country without any of my things—no hairbrush, no make-up, no sunscreen or toothpaste. Since I was dressed in winter clothes, what would I wear tomorrow in the tropical heat? Woo-woo-woo! I thought the trip was ruined.

A good night's sleep helped me gain some perspective. The next morning, we set out to gather some supplies and discovered that even in Costa Rica there is shopping. Duh! It wasn't quite like the department stores I was familiar with, but they had everything we needed. It turned out to be a lot of fun picking out tourist outfits and toothbrushes.

This experience, while I did not choose it, taught me that I can cope with unexpected changes better than I thought. I will never forget my first two days in Costa Rica.

Is planning and preparation your superpower? If so, the unexpected is your kryptonite. Tomorrow, we'll begin to build some immunity.

18

Underplan, Underprepare!

Today, we're going to cut our planning and preparing time in half. Whether it's planning for a vacation, preparing for a meeting, or just making a shopping list, we're going to do it twice as quickly as usual. If you would typically take an hour to pack for a weekend away, pack your bags in thirty minutes. If you normally take ten minutes to put together an outfit for work, this morning, dress yourself in five.

 For those of us who love to plan and prepare, it can feel relaxing to sit for an hour with a pencil and paper brainstorming everything we need to do for an upcoming task or event. That's because the monkey mind likes to see us doing something about the uncertain future and rewards us with rest-and-digest sensations and emotions so long as we keep it up. It wants a favorable outcome no matter how much time and effort it costs us. And while a certain amount of planning is necessary in life, when we feel it's necessary or even possible to be ready for every contingency and eliminate every risk, we are serving the monkey, not our higher self. When we believe the mind-set that says, *Being totally prepared is the only way I can relax,* we can never truly relax, because there is always one more thing to prepare for. Even as we execute one plan successfully, we are planning for the next in our heads.

What's more, if our plans and preparations are successful and there are no surprises, our resilience to difficulty atrophies, just like a muscle that is underused. Without resilience, we are fragile and unprepared for the universal uncertainty of life.

The new expansive mind-set we are adopting is *Since I can't plan and prepare for everything, I want to be practice resilience.* That includes resilience to our emotions about being underprepared as well as resilience to problems we didn't plan for. Hopefully we will get practice with both. In fact, if, due to your restriction on planning and preparing today, you forget to pack a hair dryer, omit a couple of PowerPoint slides, or your boots and belt don't match, *good!* This is why we call it a workout! Whatever the result of your practice, move your wristband and give yourself some praise for adopting a new mind-set and welcoming emotion.

By allowing for some things to go wrong, to be forgotten, or to remain unfinished, we get valuable practice in learning to cope with the unexpected. In our lifetimes, all of us will have challenging experiences beyond our control, whether that be natural disasters, our own illness or that of our loved ones. This low-stakes exercise will build the muscle we need to be resilient when high-stakes adversity strikes. With resilience comes confidence that allows us to be at peace and fully present with whatever is happening around us, planned and prepared for or not.

☆ Remember not to trash yourself for not anticipating something you normally would have. When we cut our anticipation time in half, that's what is supposed to happen. Praise yourself for opening to the feeling of being underprepared.

Are you a serial expiration date checker? Do you tend to throw out food because you worry it might have gone bad? Does it make you uncomfortable to eat food other people have prepared because others are not as careful about this as you are? Tomorrow you will throw caution to the wind, not food into the trash.

19 Throw Caution, Not Food, To the Wind

Today, we will refrain from looking at expiration dates on food! If you are shopping, just assume that anything that the grocer placed on the shelf is fresh and up to date. If you are preparing food that has an expiration date on it, give it the benefit of a doubt also. And if you are eating at someone else's house, don't ask or check. The only exceptions to this throwing-out-caution exercise are infant formulas, meat, dairy, and eggs that have been in your refrigerator for a while.

You can make this exercise more difficult or less, depending on how anxious it makes you. If you're not a regular expiration date checker and you need a bigger challenge, extend the exercise to fruits and vegetables that are bruised or wilted. Conversely, if the exercise feels overwhelming, you might start by only ignoring expiration dates on items with a longer shelf life like cereals, grains, and crackers. Or you could limit the exercise to new purchases at the grocery store and continue to check dates on foods at home. But don't get out a magnifying glass or ask others to smell the food just to make sure it is okay. These reassurance-seeking behaviors will spoil the exercise.

The average American throws out one pound of food per day, a good indicator of excess caution about food freshness. Expiration dates on food are not absolute deadlines that mean the food will be unsafe to eat the day after it expires.

The terms "Best by" or "Use by" are conservative estimates of when foods will taste best, not dates after which you will get horribly sick or die. If you don't consume food unless you've checked the expiration date, you are operating under the monkey mind-set *If I can't confirm the food I eat is 100% safe, I am in danger.* This not only leads to a lot of wasted food, it feeds the belief that the world is more dangerous than it is. It prevents us from taking reasonable risks and reinforces that we cannot trust the world, others, and our own bodies.

Of course, the monkey mind won't let us do this exercise without some pushback. When we resist the impulse to toss out "expired" food today, we may feel doubt and fear. When we're hijacked by the monkey, we think, *It is better to be safe than sorry. I must eliminate every possibility of getting sick.*

The expansive mind-set we are feeding today is *I don't need to be 100% certain about food expiration dates to be safe.* The anxiety we're going to feel while resisting the urge to check dates or to toss out slightly bruised fruit is growing pain. We're growing coping skills, flexibility and confidence. Use your welcoming muscles and breathe into your sensations, creating lots of space around them in your body for them to play themselves out. While there are no expiration dates on emotions, we know they don't last forever!

This exercise is about so much more expiration dates or bruised fruit. Courage is the value we're after today, the courage we need to take reasonable risks. When we move outside of our comfort zone of certainty, even in low-risk situations like pouring a glass of milk or opening a can of beans, we are learning to tolerate the discomfort that prevents us from taking risks in other, higher-risk areas of our lives. Whether you are after success at work or relaxation in the kitchen, having risk tolerance is essential. Remember, the world is not as dangerous as our monkey mind would lead us to believe.

For regular expiration date checkers, this habit can be a tough one to break. Be sure to move your wristband every time you resist the urge to check, welcome your anxiety, and redirect your to your expansive mind-set. And if you couldn't muster the courage today, don't give up. Try again tomorrow, lowering the bar a little. Time doesn't stop, so there will always be new "Use by" dates to practice on!

The other day I took a seat at a meeting next to an out-of-town colleague who had driven fifty miles to be there. As we were exchanging pleasantries, she happened to mention that she had forgotten her purse. "I drove extra carefully so as not to get pulled over," she said with a chuckle. "And I may have to borrow money for lunch." Then she let out a laugh and added, "I'm just happy I remembered my cell phone!" I was struck by her easygoing attitude despite forgetting something so essential.

We all forget things occasionally, and our typical reaction is often to judge ourselves harshly, vowing to be more vigilant in the future. If my friend had done this, how tedious it might have been for me to listen to her story, and telling it wouldn't have helped her remember better next time. Instead, she was a perfect model of an expanded mind-set in action—someone who could relax and laugh in the face of inconvenience and uncertainty at leaving her purse and wallet behind. Buying her lunch was a small price to pay for the inspiration she provided!

Do you worry about forgetting things? Tomorrow, we are going to question our need for certainty that we have everything we need!

20

Forget About It

Whenever we make an exit today, we'll refrain from trying to remember everything we might want to take along. When we leave home, for example, instead of scanning our surroundings to make sure we aren't leaving something behind or checking off mental lists of everything we need, we'll just grab and go. Wherever you are going—to work, to play, or to run errands, the protocol is the same: leave without reviewing, whether you think you have remembered everything or not!

(*Caveat*: If today is the day of your multimedia presentation to the board or the marathon you've been training for, choose another exercise. Keep this a low-stakes exercise!)

Like many of the exercises in this book, this one may seem foolish. What's wrong with trying to ensure we have everything with us that we are likely to need? Don't we have enough problems in our lives already?

Bringing along things we'll need when we go somewhere is wise, but if we feel stressed and anxious about whether we've got *every*thing, we perpetuate a cycle of fear: the more we try to remember everything, the more afraid we are of forgetting something. This monkey feeding doesn't prepare us for the inevitable moment when we forget our purse or discover we also need an umbrella—moments where we need to be flexible and creative. When that happens, we are lost. We don't know how to improvise. We come to believe that *I must anticipate everything I'm going to need, or my day will be ruined!*

The expansive mind-set we want to create is *If I forget something I need, I can cope.* The way we cultivate this mind-set is to have the experience of *not* being totally prepared and then to successfully cope with it. Of course, this coping experience won't happen without opposition from our limbic alarm system. Paying less attention to what we've packed will make us feel more anxious. We'll be afraid of leaving, afraid we'll have to turn back, and afraid we won't be able to do without whatever we may have forgotten. Welcome all these feelings. Our intention is to let them be, and then go about our business. Remember to praise yourself for it too.

If we do forget something essential, we may well experience some shame as well as disappointment and anger with ourselves. If you feel this way, remind yourself that forgetting something is part of the exercise and not a sign you have done something wrong; this is a great opportunity to cultivate self-compassion.

When we stop reviewing mental lists and double-checking every time we exit a location, we can be more spontaneous in our comings and goings. When we do forget something, it's an opportunity to tap into our underutilized creativity and problem-solving skills. (Ever use a garbage bag for a raincoat?) When we can trust in our ability to improvise, we won't have to turn around every time we remember that we forgot something. The freer we are of the illusion that we can ever be totally prepared for everything ahead, the more relaxed and confident we will be moving forward.

Don't get fooled. This exercise is not intended to prove you don't need mental lists or double-checking. It's designed to teach you to welcome the experience of not being sure that you have everything you need. That is all!

Do you agonize over making decisions because you're not certain how they will turn out? Tomorrow, we'll learn how to change the way we choose, as well as how to live with the decisions we make.

21

Make a Quick Decision

Today, we will make a decision without being certain it is right. There are three things you can do in this exercise; you can do one or all three. It's up to you.

1. Set the timer for five minutes and write out pros and cons of your options.

2. Set the timer for one minute to make the decision (Base it on the pros and cons, or just go with your gut.)

3. If the timer goes off and you haven't decided, flip a coin to decide.

It is probably best to stick with a low-stakes decision like whether to eat out or in, but the protocol will work on big decisions too. What's important is that you trigger a level of discomfort that does not overwhelm you.

Most choices in life are of the apples-or-oranges variety; each has advantages and disadvantages. And since we can't predict the future, no amount of thought will bring complete assurance whether an apple or an orange will nourish us the best tomorrow. Yet we unconsciously believe there's always a "right" choice, and if we aren't sure what that right choice is, we feel uncomfortable and afraid. We go back and forth between our options, hoping we can guess "correctly."

To the monkey mind, every choice is evaluated in terms only of survival. Any choice that could potentially threaten our happiness and well-being—and almost any choice will—triggers a limbic system alarm telling us *Woo-woo-woo! Too dangerous. Don't choose that!* Hijacked by emotion, we are unable to tap into the higher values that would better guide our decisions, values like courage, trust, acceptance, and creativity. By choosing on the side of safety—or postponing choosing—we miss out on new experiences where we can grow. We come to believe that *I must be 100 percent certain of my decision. If I make a wrong choice, I might not recover.*

This exercise will teach us to tolerate the negative emotions that arise with decisions so they don't dictate what we decide. By sticking with the three-step protocol given above, we put the apples-and-oranges debate aside and step into the unknown, free of any illusions that we can be 100 percent certain about our choice. Only in this new territory can we both enjoy the benefits of the upside of our decision and also learn to cope with the downside. Coping—being flexible, creative, and resilient—is the best insurance we can have against "bad" decisions. As we learn how to cope, we gain confidence that whatever decision we make—even those we make quickly—will move us forward. The expansive mind-set we are practicing is *I don't need to be certain I am making the right decision because I can cope with any outcome.* Be sure to praise yourself—move that wristband—every chance you get.

Any relief we might feel that we are making the "right" decision is fragile and temporary. The future will always surprise us. Far better is the confidence that we can handle the downside of any choice we make. With this kind of confidence, there is no such thing as a wrong decision!

Watch out for judging whether the choice you made wound up being the best. The only wrong decision in this exercise is the one you make in which you don't welcome the outcome and miss out on practicing coping skills. Feeling the pain of uncertainty and reminding yourself of your expansive mind-set are what we're after, and what you reward yourself for.

My husband, Doug, shares this story. *Last year, after much painful deliberation, I signed up for a fourteen-day silent meditation retreat in an isolated temple in the mountains of Colorado. There would be no internet, spotty cell coverage, and no digital devices. But I decided to hedge my bet on my personal growth and sneak my phone in. I told myself, I need to check my emails at least once a day. I didn't feel too bad about this compromise; fortunately, Tibetan Buddhists don't believe in sin.*

For twenty-three hours, forty-five minutes a day, I left my phone tucked under my pillow, waiting for the fifteen minutes I allowed myself to check on the outside world. What I noticed the first few days was that without my phone holstered in my pocket, the urge to whip it out wasn't as strong as usual. The monkey was learning amazingly quickly that there was no use prompting me to check on news that wasn't available. The next thing I noticed was that when I did check, there wasn't that much of importance going on.

I could easily sort through my emails and the latest news in fifteen minutes.

By day four, I was scanning subject and headlines only, and on the Sunday at the end of the first week, I forgot to check my phone at all. For the rest of the retreat, I had a completely different relationship with my phone. It felt like an ex-lover, someone I didn't necessarily want to run into all the time.

When the departure day arrived, on the shuttle bus, the phone in my right front pocket felt unfamiliar and heavy. Nearing the airport, I noticed that I didn't want to turn it on to confirm my flight time. I felt a little curious about what had happened in the world while I was gone, but the idea of booting up felt like an intrusion into my life, an obligation more than anything else. Over the next few hours and days, as I used my phone more and more, an old familiar phenomenon began to return—urges. I recognized that every time I checked my email, messages, texts, and news feeds, I was training the monkey. Everything my unconscious mind had unlearned at the retreat was being relearned.

Understanding how quickly I can condition myself into and out of a habit has been a revelation to me. Every time I feel the urge to check what's happening out there, I can choose instead to check what's happening right here and now. I don't need to be in a meditation retreat to make a mindful choice.

Are you frequently interrupted by texts, emails, and social media throughout your day? Whether you are trying to work, play, or relax, monitoring incoming alerts and notifications can be a problem. Tomorrow, we'll try a different approach.

Go Off the Grid

22

Our exercise today is to set aside a designated period of time where we will choose to turn off our phones—or put them in airplane mode—and disable the Wi-Fi on our computers. We'll be offline, out of touch, in a world of our own. How long you will be disconnected is up to you, but you will want the length of time to be suitably challenging. For some, an hour will feel overwhelming; for others, it might take an entire afternoon to feel the loss of connection. Whatever length of time you choose, stick to it.

Some of us can remember a time when we put a letter in the mailbox, feeling quite comfortable with the prospect of receiving a reply in a few weeks. We'd return from a day at work, a weekend trip, or even a week-long vacation and check our message machine to see who called, and if there was anything we felt was important enough, we might return the call sometime during the next couple of days. How relaxed and confident we were that the world could wait for us!

With the development of the internet, we have slowly conditioned ourselves to feel like first responders, on call 24/7. *What if this call is important? The email I don't read right away might be time sensitive. What if they are waiting for a reply to this text? What if there is an emergency or an accident?* The adrenaline and dopamine flooding our limbic system are the call to action of the monkey mind. *Woo-woo-woo! Pick up your phone and find out!* And every time we pick up the phone, we reinforce the belief that the only way we can cope with the future is to be fully informed as it unfolds, every minute of the day! Our mind-set is *It is not safe to ignore incoming messages. I need to be certain about every opportunity or threat!*

Even if certainty were attainable, serving the monkey by being on call is too high a price to pay. Eliminating the flow of alerts and notifications is the most powerful way to train the monkey that we are in charge, that the moment we are experiencing is more important than our need to know. By turning off the spigot, we serve notice that we are off duty and have a right to peace and calm.

When we become anxious, bored, agitated, lonely, or even afraid during our time offline today, we will remind ourselves that negative emotions are not a valid cause for action. Our mind-set is *I can address incoming messages only at a designated time and cope with the consequences.* We survived without the grid for thousands of years; we can make it through our lunch break! Our job is to fully experience the loss of the instant gratification the grid has fostered, to accept the feelings that accompany that loss and indeed to welcome them. Every time you do, move your wristband to remind yourself that you are giving your best to this exercise.

As we free ourselves us from our on-call status and state of hyperarousal, we build confidence in our ability to work, play, and rest at our own pace. This self-confidence is what allows us to feel at peace, whether we've seen the latest incoming text message, email, phone call, or not.

A wonderful side effect of this practice is more productivity, flow, and creativity. Why? Studies have shown that even a two-second glance at our phones interrupts our performance on cognitive tasks, increases mistakes, and decreases productivity. Who knows what you are capable of when you go off the grid?

This exercise is not meant to demonstrate that nothing terrible will happen if you go offline for a while, so you get no points for discovering that. We reward ourselves for how completely we welcomed the feelings of withdrawal from the grid and how often we reviewed our expansive mind-set.

Are you a serial checker-upper on your children, your mate, or other loved ones? When they're out of sight, is it easy for you to assume the worst? Tomorrow, we'll try assuming the best for a bit.

Loosen Grip on Loved Ones **23**

Today's exercise is to reduce or, better yet, eliminate checking up on loved ones. We will operate with the assumption that unless we hear otherwise, our loved ones are safe and secure. This will be tough for those of us accustomed to receiving regular reassurance throughout the day that our children, our mates, our parents, or our friends have arrived safely, are healthy, still like us, or simply are having a good day. If you can't give checking up altogether, set a goal to cut checking on others in half or by 25 percent, or try to delay checking for five or ten minutes every time you get the urge.

Note: Sometimes your loved ones are also anxious and/or trained to give you a lot of reassurance. You will need to let them know this is what you are working on and ask them to refrain from reassuring you.

Anxiety about our loved ones is a call to action from the monkey mind. When we react by checking, we get temporary relief from that anxiety, but at a high price. Every time we check, we condition ourselves to think they could be in danger. This means more calls to action—*Woo-woo! Check and make sure!*—in the future. We come to believe *Anything could happen with my loved ones; I won't feel safe unless I am sure.*

By *not* checking on our loved ones when we have the urge to check, we will trigger heightened anxiety for their safety and well-being as well as our own. Welcome these feelings with your breath, knowing they will eventually pass. So long as we continue not to check, we are training the monkey mind that the unknowns in the lives of our family and social circle can stay unknown. And we'll be training ourselves to think differently, to believe that *I can assume my loved ones are safe unless there are clear signs of danger. I don't need to check.*

Remember, every time you don't check when you have the urge, welcome an uncomfortable emotion, or redirect your mind-set, move your wristband!

By checking on our loved ones less often, we will develop a more realistic view of the dangers to their well-being as well as to our own. They won't be interrupted by our need for confirmation that they are okay or that they still love us, which can be annoying and cause resentment. And by not overchecking on our children, we won't be modeling behaviors that make them more anxious.

The more we ignore our urges to check, the fewer urges we will get. Perhaps more importantly, instead of being constantly distracted by concerns for others, we'll feel confident enough to focus our attention on what's happening for *us* right here and now.

⭐ Don't judge today's exercise by how well your loved ones did without you checking. What deserves your attention and your praise is how much you welcomed the feeling of not knowing how they were doing and how you redirected yourself to your expansive *I don't need to know* mind-set.

Once a year at my gym, there is a special kind of competition. On the face of it, it doesn't make a whole lot of sense. Participating members sign up for teams, and the team that goes to the most classes wins. That means to be competitive, we had to attend classes we wouldn't normally attend. Frankly, that didn't interest me. Why would I want to embarrass myself trying Zumba when I could demonstrate my mastery in my regular muscle class? And how likely was I to get a satisfying workout in a yoga class?

Then one year, a couple of my Pilates class members turned on the peer pressure and, against my better judgment, I gave in and signed up. For the next month, I took classes I did not even know were offered, stepping into African dance studio, plunging into water aerobics class, and leaning in to extreme core sessions. It wasn't always pretty. I discovered that I could hurt myself kickboxing—by pulling a hamstring—far worse than I could hurt anyone else. While Yamuna body rolling— lying down on rock-hard balls to deeply stretch your muscles—I discovered a flavor of physical pain I had never encountered. Every class that was new to me, whether it was physically challenging, painful or not, required new skills and took me out of my normal comfort zone.

I can't say that I excelled in any of the new classes I took that month, and my team didn't win, but the purpose of the competition was to create a playful way to break us out of our rigid exercise habits, and at that I succeeded. I discovered that I could survive classes where I don't know what will be required of me. I learned I don't have to have any natural aptitude at something to do it. I gained a ton of confidence in my own resilience that month, and that confidence has translated into a stronger sense of belonging and presence in the gym at large. Plus, I discovered Zumba!

Does it feel like Groundhog Day when you wake up in the morning? Are you a creature of habit? Would you like a little more spice in life?

24 Rock Your Routine

Identify a predictable default behavior today, and change it. If you usually eat out for lunch, pack one today. If you have an exercise routine, try a new class or a different piece of equipment at the gym. If you always shower, take a bath. If you typically watch TV at night, then read a book, go out to a movie, or monitor the night sky for comets.

We like to rationalize our tried-and-true routines as efficient. They keep us from wasting time doing things that don't work. But they also keep us from experiencing new things that make life fresh and interesting. They reinforce the monkey mind-set that says, *I am only safe when I am comfortable and can predict the outcome of what I am doing.*

When we put aside our old behavior and replace it with something different today, we'll wake the monkey mind out from its comfortable slumber. We'll feel doubtful that the new behavior will be satisfying to us, anxiety about whether we will do it correctly or well, and irritation at any discomfort we face or obstacles that pop up.

This is exactly what we want to happen. We are purposely creating instability, challenging ourselves to adapt to changing conditions. Our first adaptation is to embrace our new expansive mind-set: *Flexibility is a key to confidence and greater aliveness.* Our second adaptation is to open ourselves to, rather than to resist, our negative emotions, letting the monkey exhaust itself with its false alarms. Be sure to praise yourself for these adaptations, both the mental and the physical. This is hard work!

This exercise builds flexibility, and like a tree in the wind, the more flexible we are, the more resilient we are. With resilience comes confidence, confidence that we can be spontaneous and creative, even while doing an activity we are unfamiliar with or cannot do very well. This is how we grow and learn and make a dynamic life for ourselves. This is where we discover the meaning of joy.

Remember that the point of this exercise is not to master the new activity, but rather to feel the loss of the old. If you felt uncomfortable changing your routine and continued with that change allowing that discomfort, you rocked it!

Are you in the habit of getting little reality checks throughout your day, or you comfortable leaving room for doubt? Tomorrow, we'll shine some light on what for many of us is an invisible behavior.

Recognize Reassurance Seeking

25

How often do we voice our doubts and concerns for the purpose of being reassured? Today, we are going to find out. We won't attempt to curb our reassurance-seeking behavior or change it in any way. We'll simply notice it.

Hint: For most of us, reassurance seeking is completely unconscious behavior, an automatic reflex that is triggered many times a day. To catch ourselves in the act, every time we ask anybody a question today, regardless how they answer it, we'll take a moment to ask this question of ourselves: *Did I need to know this to move forward in my day, or did I want to know because not knowing made me feel uneasy?* When anxiety rather than utility drives our need to know, we are seeking reassurance.

Distinguishing between anxiety and utility can be tricky. An innocuous question to your partner like *What are your plans for the day?* can be motivated to varying degrees by both anxiety and utility. But if we are honest with ourselves, we will recognize when it is the monkey that is driving us to ask the question. As always, our emotions are the key.

In our personal relationships, insecurity and jealousy prompt us to seek reassurance about whether our partner is physically safe, whether they are mad at us or still love us, or whether they are attracted to someone else. Our own bodily sensations can trigger reassurance seeking: *Could this headache be an aneurysm?* And the decisions we are faced with can feel overwhelming, prompting us to ask advice about even the smallest decisions. Rumors in our work environment, alarming news events, practically any change around us can make us start asking each other, *Do you think…? Should I…? What if…?* Our mind-set is *Any doubt, uncertainty, or insecurity is a sign that I must ask!*

When there is an imminent threat, we need the best guidance. But the monkey mind cannot differentiate between what is imminently threatening, and thus actionable, and what is not, and we get lots of false alarms in the form of negative emotions. We feel slightly on edge, unable to relax completely, and we look to others to give us confidence.

We will not be resisting the urge to seek reassurance today, but we will be getting some good exercise nonetheless—mindfulness exercise. We'll be shining light on behavior we've been doing in the dark by cultivating a self-compassionate mind-set: *I can observe myself seeking reassurance without judgment or criticism.*

Don't forget to keep track of how often you seek reassurance. In the tools, you'll find a tally sheet to help you do that, but you can do it on piece of paper, in a notes app, or, if you're mathematically gifted, in your head.

This exercise fosters curiosity and objectivity, qualities from which new insight will arise. Every time we notice ourselves seeking reassurance is an opportunity to question whether it is in accordance with our higher values or whether it serves the agenda of the monkey mind.

This is first day of a two-day practice, so don't get ahead of yourself. Our work today is to notice our reassurance seeking and keep track. If you paid attention to your behavior all day and found no reassurance seeking, great! If you paid attention to your behavior all day and discovered you're a chronic reassurance seeker, also great! Either way, give yourself a pat on the back.

Picture a fourth grader in the backseat on her way to school, asking her mother, "Where will you be today?"

"I'll be at work, just like I was yesterday."

"How long will you be there?"

"All day. I work all day every day while you're at school. You know that."

"When will you come and pick me up?"

"Three-thirty, the same time I pick you up every day!"

Children with separation anxiety need a lot of reassurance; nothing their parents tell them seems to comfort them for long. When the child is caught in a cycle, the more reassurance they get, the more they need. During the first few years of my clinical practice working with highly anxious children, I was continually faced with the question of how to incentivize a child to put up with a short-term pain to get a long-term gain.

As an experiment, I decided to try using the most widely accepted incentive in human history: money. At the end of every weekly session, I instructed the parent to give the child ten one-dollar bills. Over the course of the next week, every time the child asked for reassurance about the availability or whereabouts of their parent, they would have to pay a dollar to be reassured. When their money was exhausted, no further reassurance would be given. But if the child managed to hold on to any of the money by the end of the week, there would be no limitations on how they could spend it. I was pleasantly surprised to discover that monetizing our reward system worked. Reassurance bucks soon became an essential tool in my practice.

What did this seemingly superficial solution accomplish? First, when the anxious children realized there was a price to pay every time they asked for reassurance, the anxiety cycle was interrupted. They had a moment to reconsider: How badly do I need this reassurance right now? Is it worth a dollar? Second, when they chose not to give in to the urge, they could keep their dollar—a short-term reward to counter the short-term discomfort of not being reassured. And finally, within only a few weeks most children were coming into our sessions with not only a steadily growing wad of cash but dramatically less anxiety. They morphed from clingy to confident.

As adults, we may not have the classic symptoms of separation anxiety, but if we're in the habit of reassurance seeking, we're stuck in a similar cycle, and it's one that extracts a far heftier price from us than a reassurance buck. Every time we feed the monkey, we are giving up our higher values. To recognize the incentive, we have to break this cycle. To do this, we might ask ourselves, How much more confident and resilient might I be if I didn't need to rely on others to keep uncertainty at bay?

26

Reduce Reassurance Seeking

Whenever we are faced with an uncertainty today, unless it requires immediate attention, we will not seek reassurance from anyone else. Whether it's a scary news story (*Could that happen here?*), a sudden unexplained pain (*Am I getting sick?*), or doubt about a decision you made (*Is this a good decision?*), we will resist the impulse to consult others.

When we feel anxious or insecure, it is very natural—and some might say sensible—to get someone else's opinion or to consult an authority. In instances where there is an immediate threat, we need to have access to the best guidance. But in today's complex environment, we are inundated with data of all kinds, most of which does not indicate an immediate threat and, as such, does not require action.

When we use reassurance to dampen the feelings that accompany every possible eventuality— even those that are unlikely, remote, or beyond our control—we never learn how to tolerate multiple possibilities in our future. We never get a chance to prove to ourselves—and prove to that hairy little security guard in our brain—that we can handle not knowing for sure how things will turn out. The monkey grows ever more vigilant, looking for more and more instances where we might be heading toward danger.

At every dip of the market, we ask others what they think, watch TV analysts, or call our broker. With every change in our skin tone or blood pressure, we consult loved ones or call our doctor. Every natural disaster anywhere in the world prompts the question *Should we be worried?* We are always slightly on edge, unable to relax completely. We look to others to give us confidence. Our mind-set is *Any doubt, uncertainty, and insecurity is a sign that I must ask!*

By resisting the urge to seek reassurance, we exercise the welcoming muscle, allowing our feelings of anxiety and doubt to simply be. When these feelings are welcomed and given space to play out, they do not persist for long. From beginning to end, any emotion that goes unresisted lasts only minutes, not hours. The more we do this exercise, the more efficiently these feelings will cycle through in the future, and our need for reassurance will diminish. And as that need diminishes, our self-confidence grows. We come to believe in our own judgment, recognizing that most of the monkey's alarms don't need a response and that we can take appropriate action when necessary.

Moving forward without reassurance puts us in new territory where risk is an acceptable feature of the landscape. With each step, we gain a deeper sense of autonomy and confidence. We begin to think in a new way: *By not seeking reassurance from others, I am cultivating trust and confidence in myself.* Acknowledge this new way of thinking by moving your wristband.

☀ Without fail, when my clients reduce the reassurance they ask for, their anxiety and need to be certain reduces accordingly, their confidence in themselves grows, and their ability to experience what's happening "here and now" increases. This exercise will do the same for you!

⭐ When we don't get reassurance about something that we want to be reassured about, it often turns out afterward that there was no threat after all and thus no real need for reassurance. While this is a nice discovery, it is not the rationale for the exercise and you get no points for that. Our mission is (1) to feel the feelings that arise when we are not reassured and (2) to remind ourselves again and again of our new expansive mind-set.

Are you agenda driven? Is your day naturally orderly and predictable? Tomorrow, we're going to play our hand a little differently.

27

Shuffle Your Deck

Whenever possible today, leave the order of things you do to chance. This is a good practice to do on a day off. Most of us have a general idea of what we are going to do each day, and we have a habit of doing those things in a certain order. Today, we will disrupt the order. The best way to do this is to write down two to six things on separate slips of paper. For example, I just wrote down three things—take a shower, write this exercise, make a cup of coffee—all things I wanted to do. After writing them down, I shuffled the pieces of paper, put them in a pile, and did whatever activity was on the top. The first card I pulled was to make coffee, the second was to take a shower, and the third was to write this exercise. This is the order I followed.

Our limbic system is programmed to prevent chaos and to promote order and predictability. The monkey mindset is *I must optimize my time by doing things in the correct familiar routine.* But if keeping things safe and predictable is our only value, we are likely to plan each day the same way we planned the day before. Over time, we get more rigidly attached to what is familiar and less resilient when something unexpected arises.

By purposely discarding our efficient, orderly, routine approach to planning today, we are inviting in a little chaos. This means we'll be inviting some negative emotions as well, and allowing them lots of space to work themselves out. We'll do this with our welcoming breath and by returning again and again to our new *expansive* mind-set: *By doing things in random order, I am learning to be more flexible and resilient.* Then move your wristband to remind yourself what a good job you're doing!

Doing things in random order helps us to develop more flexibility, creativity, and confidence. With these qualities, on future occasions when our routine is disrupted by things beyond our control, we can respond with resilience and grace.

Remember to focus on the process, not the outcome. This practice is about changing your routine, regardless whether it was efficient, whether you liked it, or whether you got everything done you had planned. Welcoming whatever happens is our only purpose.

All through my marriage whenever my family went on vacation, I did the planning. I like planning things. I don't 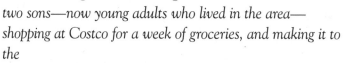 *mind doing the work up front that will make things go smoothly for everyone. So, with family vacations I let my husband stick to the driving, the kids stick to their music and podcasts, while I stuck to what I do best.*

A couple years ago, my husband, sons, daughter, and I were all going on a family vacation to Orcas Island off the coast of Washington State. Among other things, the trip required a ferry ride with a complex schedule, mandatory reservations, and long queues of cars competing for limited space on the boat. The logistics of flying into Seattle, renting a car, collecting our two sons—now young adults who lived in the area— shopping at Costco for a week of groceries, and making it to the ferry on time felt like too big a job for anyone but me.

But I was trying to practice what I preach about needing certainty, and during the flight, I decided that  *when we hit the ground in Seattle, I would step into the unknown. At the baggage claim, I announced to my husband and daughter that I was delegating* planning to whoever wanted it. I was going to sit back and let go of control. You should have seen their faces!

Well, I can't say it was easy. I kept thinking, If we miss the ferry, we won't be able to get to the island and the trip will be ruined! The periodic waves of anxiety felt like I was going to be being carsick. But I rode them out. And as it turned out, my family was up to the task; we made it to the ferry on time. But that's not the point of the story. What I got out of the experience was a taste of freedom.

I can plan, sure, but I can also be planned for. Even as I write this, it feels pretty new, but that's understandable. I have a life-long planning habit to break and lots of delegating practice ahead of me!

Are you most comfortable when you're in charge? Do you have difficulty appreciating how others do things, and feel like you're the only one that gets results? Tomorrow, there will be a change of leadership.

28  Don't DIY, Delegate!

Think of a task that you feel only you can do well or that you almost always do. Today, you are going to entrust that task to someone else who might not deliver the same results.

Typical examples include creating a meeting agenda or planning a lunch with a coworker, a night out with your family or partner, a party or another informal gathering. Rather than seizing the reins with this event, ask someone else to lead. Once you've delegated responsibility, allow your stand-in complete freedom to make decisions—no subtle hints of how *you* would be doing it or second-guessing their decisions, even if it requires duct taping your mouth! (*Note:* I'm not suggesting you turn over your entire wedding planning to your sister. But you might ask her to choose the photographer or the DJ.)

The monkey mind-set we are targeting with this exercise is this: *To secure a desired outcome, I must do the task myself.* While our ability to plan and act effectively is a valuable skill, it can get in the way of being more relaxed and easygoing. Meanwhile, our distrust of others' abilities does not go unnoticed; our friends and coworkers may feel patronized and resentful.

The expansive mind-set we want to foster is *Regardless of how others do this task, I can cope.* To believe this about ourselves, we need to get some experience allowing others to lead and try our hand at coping with the results. This exercise will create that experience. We're going to watch someone else do things their way, not ours. We're going to feel fear, apprehension, and insecurity—emotions we usually try to avoid.

To dampen these feelings, our impulse will be to worry whether the delegate is doing it right, second-guessing everything they do, and sneaking in helpful advice to steer them in the direction we want to go. If you don't like how the person does things, there will also be a strong urge to point this out, correct them, or express disappointment. Before we begin this exercise, we will create a clear intention to resist those impulses. We will employ our new expansive mind-set and welcome the feelings with open arms, giving them as much room as they need to play themselves out. And when we do these things, we'll give ourselves a little acknowledgment by moving our wristband!

Delegating tasks to others gives us a chance to take a breather from needing to be in control. It teaches us to be flexible, patient, and respectful toward others, and—should their planning and/or execution not work so well—to be compassionate, creative, and resilient. Over time, your welcoming muscle will be strong enough to flex no matter who's in charge!

☆ There will be a natural tendency to judge our experience by how well it worked out. If your delegating worked out well for everyone, that's fine. If it was a disaster, that is also fine. Either way, your mission was the same—to create a new experience to build resilience to emotions that were limiting you.

When faced with a choice, do you get stressed about making the right decision or do you tend to go with what is most predictable? Tomorrow, you're going to surprise yourself!

Flip a Coin

Look for situations today where you have a choice between two options. Then choose by flipping a coin. Whatever choice we make—the scarf or the necklace, regular lettuce or organic, Netflix or a book—we'll make it a heads-or-tails decision.

Note: Keep it to low-stakes choices only. We're not going to choose a career or a life partner with a coin!

Whenever we have two options, and our tolerance for uncertainty is low, we become stressed about making the "right" choice. Our mind-set is *I must make good decisions to make sure nothing bad happens.* Because we tend to make choices that are safe and predictable, we don't get a chance to develop resilience to challenging outcomes. When we make a choice that turns out badly, we punish ourselves, which reinforces our stress the next time we're faced with a decision.

When we flip a coin to make a decision, we give up any illusion of control over the outcome. We're adopting a playful approach that allows us to learn to cope with whatever happens. Of course, even in low-stakes situations, the monkey mind will object. We are likely to feel doubt, anxiety, and even irritation at losing control over the decision. If, for example, heads meant reading a book instead of streaming a movie, we might easily think, *This takes too much effort. After a hard day of work, I just need to zone out.*

Whether we feel anxiety, doubt, or irritation by our heads-or-tails decision, we will breathe the feeling in and make room for it. We know that nothing seriously bad will happen to us in this exercise—and we have much to gain. Rather than feeding the monkey, we are feeding our higher self, practicing our new mind-set: *By leaving this choice up to chance, I am learning how to cope with either outcome.* And as always, reward your efforts by moving your wristband!

The coping skills we are learning start with resilience to the negative emotions we're feeling about our coin-toss choice. Straying outside our comfort zone, we're learning to be flexible and spontaneous. If obstacles appear, we'll learn creative ways to get over or around them. And should the choice we left to chance disappoint us in the end, we'll learn to cope with regret. The more skilled we are at coping, the more prepared we'll be for the future. By surrendering control of our choices in mind, body, and action, ultimately we will gain genuine confidence that we can handle what is beyond our control.

⭐ Don't judge your work in this exercise by whether the choice you made by chance turned out to be the best or not. Grade yourself by how willingly you gave up control and welcomed everything that unfolded.

My client Nancy had recently bought a house with her partner, and now she was worried about the real estate market. "Nothing is selling, and I keep hearing about values going down," she told me. "It's just so upsetting to me."

"Okay," I asked her, "What is the very worst that could happen to the real estate market?"

"It may have topped out," Nancy answered. "Every house could lose half its value in the next year."

"And if that happens what would that mean about you and your future?" I asked her.

"We'd be underwater," she replied, "We'd owe the bank more than the house was worth!"

"And if that happens, what would that mean about you and your future?"

"If there was a recession and one of us got laid off, we couldn't make the payments and we'd wind up on the street!"

I pulled out a piece of paper and wrote down her words exactly, underlining "we'd wind up on the street." Then I handed her the paper.

"Okay," I said, pulling out my phone. "I'm setting the timer. For the next ten minutes, I want you to read these words out loud to yourself over and over."

Poor Nancy! She looked at me like I was crazy. Was I?

Have people ever called you a worry wart? Do you tend to imagine the worst possible outcome? Do your worries keep you up at night or distracted during the day? If so, tomorrow you are going to take charge of your worries, instead of them being in charge of you!

Welcome a Worry

Think of something you are worried about in your life right now and set aside twelve minutes to devote to it. While this may sound like an instruction to do some more worrying about whatever problem is at hand, but in reality it is an invitation to fully experience, rather than resist, the emotions that are driving our worry. To help us do that, first we'll set a timer for two minutes, during which we'll write out a short "worry script" that answers these two questions:

1. What is the very worst that might happen?

2. If it were to come true, what would it mean about me, my life, my future?

Then we'll reset the timer for ten minutes. During these ten minutes, we will read our script aloud repeatedly and welcome whatever feelings arise. Sound crazy? Maybe. But it's a crazy effective exercise nevertheless.

People often mistake worry as a feeling, when in fact it is a behavior. It is a mental ritual that we use in hope of attaining certainty, but it seldom does that for us. What this ritual *does* do is answer the call to action of the monkey mind: *Woo-woo-woo, something is wrong! Do something!* As long as we're worrying, we're doing something, which puts a cap on the negative emotion our limbic system might deliver otherwise.

It's a transaction that keeps us spinning our wheels, deepening a rut of anxiety that is hard to get out of. Every time we answer the call by worrying, we feed this mind-set: *What I don't know for certain could be catastrophic. I need to prevent the worst from happening.*

Our expansive response to what concerns us is to just keep imagining the worst. Our feelings may get very intense. Concern for the safety or well-being of loved ones, problems with our boss or our career, health issues, and political and ecological conditions all have high-stakes potential that can trigger anxiety, irritation, insecurity, fear, panic, sadness, and loss. Whatever arises, breathe into it. Don't defend yourself. We're not trying to fix these feelings or the situation that triggered them. They are like boiling water, loud and painful, but destined to evaporate into the air.

During the ten minutes, stick with your script as much as possible. Afterward, take a moment to review your new expansive mind-set regarding worry: *By accepting uncertainty, I open myself up to live more fully in the present moment.*

Every time you're tempted to worry about that problem later, day or night, thank the monkey politely and tell yourself that you will worry about it during your next scheduled worry time. Then go ahead and schedule one! It may take a few sessions, but you'll soon be surprised to discover that it becomes increasingly difficult to worry about something when you've already accepted the worst that could happen and can handle the feeling of it. And remember that your accepting and handling efforts deserve to be praised. Move your wristband with every welcomed worry.

We waste so many precious moments on earth worrying about what might go wrong in the future. By building resilience to the emotions that are driving our urge to worry, we disarm the monkey and free ourselves up to be relaxed and confident with what is, including the parts we are uncertain about. And the less energy we spend spinning our wheels with worry, the more strength we'll have to cope with the small percentage of times the worst does happen.

People often find that it is hard to stay anxious with this practice. If this happens, allow the feelings to fade just as you allowed them to intensify. They may be gone for a while only, or gone for good. No matter. Our job today is to welcome a worry.

Epilogue

Congratulations for your willingness to take this journey! I encourage you to retake the *Intolerance for Uncertainty Quiz* (http://www.monkeymindbooks.com/u). Hopefully, you will notice a change not only in your quiz score but also in your life.

To recap, here are the gains you can expect after doing these exercises.

With more resilience to negative emotions, you'll experience *more relaxation*.

With more tolerance of the unknown, you can *live life more fully in the moment*.

Assuming safety for yourself and loved ones builds *more trust in yourself, others, and the world*.

Letting go of things going as planned inspires *more confidence, flexibility, creativity, spontaneity, and joy*.

Giving up being constantly on guard allows for *the appreciation of the beauty and goodness that surrounds us*.

But please remember that psychological change is just like physical change. We need to keep exercising to maintain our gains. If you did a new exercise program for a month, you'd build muscle and stamina. But if you stopped after one month, those gains would be lost and your body would go back to its original state. I encourage you to make these exercises part of your daily life in order to not only maintain the gains you have already made, but also to continue to reap the many benefits of learning to tolerate uncertainty. How much more joy, spontaneity, trust, courage, peace, and happiness do you want? By continuously welcoming uncertainty, there's no limit, so *don't forget your daily sweat!*

Jennifer Shannon, LMFT, is author of *Don't Feed the Monkey Mind*, *The Shyness and Social Anxiety Workbook for Teens*, *The Anxiety Survival Guide for Teens*, and *A Teen's Guide to Getting Stuff Done*. She cofounded the Santa Rosa Center for Cognitive-Behavioral Therapy in Santa Rosa, CA. She is a diplomate of the Academy of Cognitive Therapy.

Foreword writer **Michael A. Tompkins, PhD, ABPP**, is a licensed psychologist who is board certified in behavioral and cognitive psychology. He is codirector of the San Francisco Bay Area Center for Cognitive Therapy.